SHO

Anupama Ch..pondent with *India Today* magazine and writes extensively about film. She has done a Masters in Journalism from Northwestern University.

Anupama currently lives in Mumbai with her husband, filmmaker Vidhu Vinod Chopra, and son, Agni.

SHOLAY

THE MAKING OF A CLASSIC

ANUPAMA CHOPRA

PENGUIN BOOKS

PENGUIN BOOKS
Published by the Penguin Group
Penguin Books India Pvt Ltd, 11 Community Centre, Panchsheel Park, New
Delhi 110 017, India
Penguin Group (USA) Inc., 375 Hudson Street, New York, New York 10014,
USA
Penguin Group (Canada), 90 Eglinton Avenue East, Suite 700, Toronto, Ontario,
M4P 2Y3, Canada (a division of Pearson Penguin Canada Inc.)
Penguin Books Ltd, 80 Strand, London WC2R 0RL, England
Penguin Ireland, 25 St Stephen's Green, Dublin 2, Ireland (a division of Penguin
Books Ltd)
Penguin Group (Australia), 250 Camberwell Road, Camberwell, Victoria 3124,
Australia (a division of Pearson Australia Group Pty Ltd)
Penguin Group (NZ), cnr Airborne and Rosedale Roads, Albany, Auckland
1310, New Zealand (a division of Pearson New Zealand Ltd)
Penguin Group (South Africa) (Pty) Ltd, 24 Sturdee Avenue, Rosebank,
Johannesburg 2196, South Africa

Penguin Books Ltd, Registered Offices: 80 Strand, London WC2R 0RL, England

First published by Penguin Books India 2000

Text copyright © Anupama Chopra 2000
Photographs copyright © Ramesh Sippy 2000

10 9 8 7 6

Typeset in Sabon by Mantra Virtual Services, New Delhi
Printed at Saurabh Printers Pvt. Ltd, Noida

For
my parents, Navin and Kamna,
and
my husband, Vinod
— Anupama Chopra

This book is dedicated to:
Our father, Ramesh Sippy,
whose passion and vision
brought the film to life;

each of his colleagues on the film,
who set standards of excellence
with their ability and effort;

all those who by having seen and
loved the film, time and time again,
keep the legend of Sholay *alive—*
the ultimate reward for its creators.
—Sheena, Sonya and Rohan

CONTENTS

INTRODUCTION: *KITNE AADMI THE?*   1

SHAAYAD KHATRON SE KHELNE KA SHAUK HAI MUJHE   9

LOHA LOHE KO KAATATA HAI   24

KEEMAT JO TUM CHAAHO, KAAM JO MEIN CHAAHUN   40

MUJHE GABBAR CHAAHIYE—ZINDA   54

LOHA GARAM HAI—MAAR DO HATHODA   62

BAHUT YAARANA LAGTA HAI   91

JO DAR GAYA, SAMJHO MAR GAYA   113

YEH HAATH NAHIN, PHAANSI KA PHANDA HAI   138

IS STORY MAIN EMOTION HAI, DRAMA HAI,
  TRAGEDY HAI   156

EPILOGUE: *YAAD RAKKHUNGA, TUJHE YAAD*
  RAKKHUNGA   179

ACKNOWLEDGEMENTS   189

INDEX   191

INTRODUCTION

KITNE AADMI THE?

Dolores Pereira was dabbing on more powder when the doorbell rang. She gave herself a once-over in the mirror: salt-and-pepper hair framed a dark, fine-boned face made grey by the film of talcum powder. Orange lipstick filled out her thin lips. A string of pearls lent a quiet dignity to her knee-length dress and closed shoes with little heels. She looked like a respectable Anglo-Indian woman going to mass somewhere in Bangalore. Actually, she was a fortune-teller getting ready for work.

Dolores was frail but feisty. In her mid-fifties, she loved to gossip. She loved to bitch. And she loved to look at male derrieres. But what made the fabulous Dolores quite exceptional was her skill with tarot cards. She would lay down the cards and foretell the future, and she had hit the bulls-eye enough times to build a widespread reputation. Dolores didn't need to advertise. Word-of-mouth alone ensured streams of Bangaloreans

1

from every walk of life at her doorstep.

That balmy evening in 1974, she opened the door to three people. One, a short man in a funny-looking floppy hat, was a film director. The second, a tall man with a beard who looked like he needed a bath, was an actor. And the third, an attractive woman with fair skin, was the actor's wife. They were making a film somewhere on the outskirts of Bangalore. They had heard a lot about Dolores. The shooting had wrapped up early that day, so they had decided to come and meet her. It was the actor's first film. He was playing a villain against a league of big stars. For him, everything hinged on this film's success. Could she please peep into their future?

Dolores spread her cards out and started to talk. The wife leaned forward, all ears. The director and actor, both a little sceptical and amused, listened too, more curious than credulous. 'This man,' Dolores said, pointing to the actor, 'is going to be right on top.' She paused dramatically, and then declared: 'And this film is going to run for many years.' The actor and the director smiled, tempted to believe but wary of doing so.

Sholay ran for five years, and changed the course of Indian cinema. And Amjad Khan became a legend—Hindi cinema's first advertising icon: Gabbar Singh, the gravelly-voiced, unwashed villain who sold both records and biscuits equally well.

*

Even Dolores could not have imagined the spectacular degree of *Sholay*'s success. The film changed lives, transformed careers, and even twenty-five years after its release it remains the box office gold standard, a reference point for both the Indian film-going audience and the film industry.

Over the years, *Sholay* has transcended its hit-movie status. It is not merely a film, it is the ultimate classic; it is

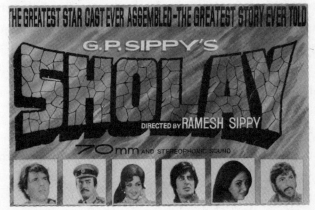

myth. It is, as director Dharmesh Darshan says, 'part of our heritage as Indians'. The characters—Veeru, Jai, Gabbar, the Thakur, Basanti and Radha—are familiar in something of the way that Ram and Sita are. The peripheral players—Soorma Bhopali, the Jailer, Kaalia and Sambha—are the stuff of folklore. Even the starring animal, Dhanno the mare, has been immortalized.

The film, still as compellingly watchable as it was when first released (in 1999 BBC-India and assorted internet polls declared it the Film of the Millennium), arouses intense passions. Its appeal cuts across barriers of geography, language, ideology and class: an advertising guru in Mumbai will speak as enthusiastically and eloquently about the film as a rickshaw driver in Hyderabad. And the devotion is often fanatical. *Sholay* connoisseurs—to call them 'fans' would be insulting their ardour—speak casually of seeing the film fifty, sixty, even seventy times. Dialogue has been memorized. Also the unique background music: the true *Sholay* buff can pre-empt all the sound effects. He can also name Gabbar's arms dealer who is on screen for less than thirty seconds (Hira), and Gabbar's father who is mentioned only once as Gabbar's sentence is read out in court ('Gabbar Singh, *vald* Hari Singh...').

Bollywood buzzes with *Sholay* stories: how a Jaipur housewife obsessed with Veeru convinced her husband to assume the name of her beloved screen hero; how Prakash bhai, a black marketeer at Delhi's Plaza Cinema, sold tickets for the film at Rs 150 for five months and eventually bought himself a small house in Seelampur, which he decorated with *Sholay* posters; how a tough-looking immigration officer in New York waved actor Macmohan through because he had seen *Sholay* and recognized Sambha, 'The man on the rock with a gun.' There are autorickshaws in Patna named Dhanno, and potent drinks in five-star bars called Gabbar.

Sholay's dialogue has now become colloquial language, part of the way a nation speaks to itself. Single lines, even phrases, taken out of context, can communicate a whole range of meaning and emotion. In canteens across the country, collegians still echo Gabbar when they notice a budding romance: '*Bahut yaarana hai.*' The lines come easily to the lips of Indians: '*Jo dar gaya, samjho mar gaya*', '*Ai chhammia*', '*Arre o Sambha*', '*Kitne aadmi the?*', '*Hum Angrezon ke zamaane ke jailer hain*'.

Predictably, *Sholay* has been used to sell everything from glucose biscuits to gripe water. And copywriters are still milking it dry. An Aiwa print advertisement, circa March 2000, ties prices for its electronic products with the run rate of the Indian cricket team, exhorting: '*Bhaag, Saurav, mere paise ka sawaal hai,*' which echoes Basanti's command to her mare: '*Bhaag, Dhanno, Basanti ki izzat ka sawaal hai.*' A Channel V filler spoofs the song '*Yeh Dosti*'. And pop star Bali Bhrambhatt makes a remix album called *Sholay 2000* and subtitled 'The Hathoda Mix', which alludes to the Thakur's lines to Veeru and Jai: '*Loha garam hai, maar do hathoda.*'

Nothing in Indian popular culture has matched this magic. Critics might argue that *Mother India* or *Mughal-e-Azam* were better films, and the trade pundits might point out that in 1994 *Hum Aapke Hain Kaun* broke *Sholay*'s box office record. But none of these films can rival *Sholay* in the scale and longevity of its success. *Sholay* was a watershed event. Director Shekhar Kapur puts it best: 'There has never been a more defining film on the Indian screen. Indian film history can be divided into *Sholay* BC and *Sholay* AD.'

There is more to Kapur's statement than just the passion of a hopeless admirer. *Sholay* is, in fact, the Indian film industry's textbook. The film married a potentially B-grade genre narrative to the big budget of a mainstream extravaganza, and taught the industry how formula can beget a classic. It changed the way Indian films looked and sounded. 'It is,' says adman and scriptwriter Piyush Pandey, 'undoubtedly the best film made in this country.' *Sholay* transformed action into high art. Stylized mayhem replaced the sissy *dhishum-dhishu*m fist fights of the past. Violence became a Hindi-movie staple for nineteen years, until *Hum Aapke Hain Kaun* flagged off the feel-good era. *Sholay* also set standards for technical excellence. Other films of the seventies seem shoddy and dated, but *Sholay* is a masterpiece of craft. To this day, directors quote *Sholay* in their films, allude to it in their frames.

The big-budget multi-starrer, where the filmmaker plays for broke, is also a legacy of *Sholay*. In its wake came endless imitations, spoofs and barely disguised remakes. The first Hindi film of the new millennium was Dharmesh Darshan's *Mela*, a multi-crore extravaganza about a girl who uses two truck drivers to avenge her brother's death at the hands of the *daku* (dacoit) Gujjar. It flopped. As did director Raj Kumar Santoshi's *China Gate* (1998), which featured ten retired army officers rescuing a village from the ferocious daku Jagira. Santoshi went blue in the face insisting that the inspiration was Akira Kurosawa's *The Seven Samurai*, but the audience didn't care. 'It's not *Sholay*,' was the verdict.

What is it about *Sholay* that works on us still? When people watch *Sholay* today, certain aspects of the film seduce them all over again: the soaring imagination of the story and the way it is told; the vitality of the scorching rocky landscape, charging horses and falling men; the gritty directorial conviction that allows an unhurried tale to be developed, full of texture and rhythm. The elements fall into place perfectly: a marvellous chemistry between the actors; a fable-like story detailed into a superb script; unforgettable dialogue and fine performances. The film skilfully blends traditional and modern elements. It has, as author Nasreen Munni Kabir says, 'Differences in lifestyles which co-exist without appearing illogical.' The steam engines, the horses, the guns and the denim give the film an ageless quality, a feeling of several centuries existing next to each other.

The morally ambiguous characters—the heroes were jean-clad mercenaries—captured the Zeitgeist of the seventies, when the idealism of the freedom struggle and the optimism of newly independent India were things of the past; when politicians and bureaucrats had lost the respect of the people, and the young had come to believe that while it was desirable to be good, it was more important to be effective. This, pretty much, is the mood even today. What appealed to audiences a quarter century ago, does so even now.

Sholay was also a film made with grand passion for a madly passionate audience. The seventies were the tail end of Hindi cinema's golden era: the film industry had the audience's undivided attention for the last time, before widespread television, videotapes, and satellites changed the entertainment landscape for ever. Producer G. P. Sippy and director Ramesh Sippy dreamed big, and they had the courage to follow their instincts. Money, market, box office—all of these commercial considerations became, in the final analysis, secondary. The prime motive was to make a mega-movie, the like of which had never been seen before on the Indian screen.

The Hollywood western, which itself had drawn lessons from Kurosawa's Japanese samurai epics, was an inspiration for both material and attitude. A sort of cowboy zeal permeated the *Sholay* unit. Ramesh and his crew were like pioneers heading out to the Wild West; warriors fighting for a just cause. They selected a barren landscape in South India, inhabited it, transformed it against mind-numbing odds to suit their vision, and created a compelling work of art. *Sholay*'s magic comes from the sweat and courage and ardour of every member of that unit. This is their story.

CHAPTER 1

SHAAYAD KHATRON SE KHELNE KA SHAUK HAI MUJHE

It was a cool January night in 1973. Amitabh Bachchan had a fever—the thermometer had read 102. His head throbbed, his face was sweaty and his mouth hot and dry. But he was at a big *filmi* party, so he smiled through clenched teeth and posed for the press photographers. When he felt faint from the strain, he lay down in the host's bedroom, though he couldn't stay there long. Making the right impression was critical. After all, he was canvassing for a role in the next G. P. Sippy production.

Amitabh had come all the way from his small suburban residence in Juhu to the imposing Shree Vijayaa Bhavan on Altamount road. G. P. Sippy, a diminutive man, was a towering figure in Bollywood: after a row of hits, he was now an A-list producer. And Amitabh, his nascent career shaky after a string of flops, badly needed work. The

Ramesh Sippy directing Hema Malini in Seeta aur Geeta

shaandar party was already in full swing when Amitabh had arrived. Sippy's terrace apartment was brimming with big industry names— distributors, directors, producers, and innumerable stars. The stars had flit in like moths to a flame, because a lead role hadn't been cast yet. The nip in the air was sharpened by the feverish expectation. There was only one question on everybody's lips: Who gets to be in Ramesh Sippy's next film?

Ramesh—G. P. Sippy's son—was launching his third film. His debut, *Andaaz*, had been a moderate success, but his second film, *Seeta aur Geeta*, released in 1972, was a box office smash hit. This *Ram aur Shyam* rip-off, in which Hema Malini essayed the double role that Dilip Kumar had played with tremendous success in the original, had already celebrated a golden jubilee and had established Hema Malini as the number one

Ramesh directing Rajesh Khanna in Andaaz.

10

heroine in Hindi cinema. The Sippys, father and son, were now looking to do something grand. They had a vaguely developed idea of an escapade-adventure film, and the word multi-starrer was being tossed around. The buzz was that the Sippys would repeat the hit *Seeta aur Geeta* team of Dharmendra and Hema Malini, but there was one more male lead. Amitabh was a contender, but the distributors seemed allergic to the actor. He was thin, morose-looking, and singularly uncharismatic. He also had ten flops behind him. *Zanjeer*, which would establish him as the new super star, hadn't yet been released.

At around midnight, the rising star of the day made a grand entry. Shatrughan Sinha cruised into the hall in his typical flamboyant fashion, just as a giant cake was being brought in. Sinha had recently had a golden run at the box office with films like *Rampur ka Laskhman* and *Bhai Ho To Aisa*. In almost all his films till then he had done the negative role of a villain, but with his unconventional looks and highly stylized acting he was attracting more fans than the heroes of the day. Everyone thronged to him. And as the flashbulbs popped, Sinha was brought centrestage. He posed with Dharamendra and Hema Malini, smiling, and slowly edged Bachchan out of the frame. As onlookers toasted the team, spontaneous applause broke out. A distributor leaned towards Ramesh and whispered into his ear: '*Yeh hai aap ki casting. Us lambuji ka sochna bhi mat.* (This is your cast. Don't even think of that tall guy.)' Ramesh only smiled.

11

*

Little about Ramesh's demeanour revealed the power he wielded. With his wiry frame and fuzzy hair, Ramesh rarely stood out in a crowd. He was a quiet man, soft-spoken and low-profile, and rarely gave interviews. In fact, on the day his film was released, he would leave town to escape the madness. He was twenty-five when he made *Andaaz* and twenty-seven when he made *Seeta aur Geeta*. The industry establishment viewed him as a bit of a brat, an upstart with a rich producer-father to bankroll

"Everybody wondered," remembers Shashi Kapoor, "Yeh Ramesh Sippy hai kya cheez?"'

his crazy ideas. 'My first film (*Andaaz*) was about a widow and a widower,' he says, 'and everyone thought I was mad.' But the audience connected with his stories. His first success was dismissed by the Bollywood bigwigs as a fluke, but the second they had to take seriously. 'Everybody wondered,' remembers Shashi Kapoor, '*Yeh Ramesh Sippy hai kya cheez?* (What is this Ramesh Sippy all about?)'

He was, quite simply, a tremendously talented storyteller. He had been dreaming about the movies since he was a little boy. As a student of St. Xavier's High School, he passed Metro cinema every day and often lingered at the crossing, looking up at the 'palace of fantasy'. His father started his first film, *Sazaa*, in 1950 and Ramesh sometimes visited the sets. Even at six, he was fascinated by the lights and the noise. His first film job came three years later, when he played Achala Sachdev's son in *Shahenshah*. He had only one line of dialogue, but the experience made a strong impression on him. 'It shook something inside me,' he recalls. 'I kept thinking about it. My grades fell in school. I was living in a different world...My mind was running away.'

Despite the falling grades, Ramesh started his college education at the prestigious London School of Economics. He spent six months struggling with a course that would earn him a degree in economics, but his heart wasn't in it. He missed the smell and the noise of the studios too much. One night he called his father and asked, 'Dad, can I come back?' A lesser man might have faltered, but G. P. Sippy was a born gambler. His answer was unequivocal: 'Yes.'

In Mumbai, Ramesh enrolled for a psychology course at Bombay University, but attended college merely to keep up the appearance of working towards a degree. His real education was in the musty production offices and studios. Every day after his morning classes finished at 9:30 a.m., he would catch a train to Kardar Studios in suburban Parel where the Sippy production office was located. He worked in both the production and direction departments in films like *Johar-Mehmood in Goa* and *Mere Sanam,* which his father was producing. His head was full of ideas. He wanted desperately to do something different. But when the eighteen-year-old son of the producer started giving too many suggestions, the *Johar-Mehmood* unit politely told him to shut up. The young man held his peace, waiting for his moment, meanwhile working as an assistant to established directors. One of his assignments was a four-day assisting stint on the hit *Mere Mehboob*. He was the seventh assistant to director H. S. Rawail. His main duty: to carry heroine Sadhna's slippers.

Somewhere in the flurry of movies, psychology got left behind. Ramesh sweated it out for seven years as an assistant before starting work on his first film, *Andaaz,* in 1969. Gulzar wrote that film. But Hema Malini, the heroine of *Andaaz,* remembers that toward the end of the shooting for the film, Ramesh was often seen huddled with two new writers, not much older than him. Their names were Salim Khan and Javed Akhtar.

*

Salim Khan wanted to be a star. The son of a police officer in Indore, he was spotted by director K. Amarnath at a wedding. Impressed by Salim's dashing good looks, Amarnath asked him to come to Mumbai and hired him as an actor for Rs 400 a month. Assorted roles followed, some lengthy, some small, but stardom remained out of reach. After seven years of struggle, Salim was still playing bit roles. 'I realized that I had the art of conception,' he says, 'but I did not have the art of projection.' At thirty, he could hardly go back home a failure. 'I would have become the laughing stock of Indore.' So he decided to put the 'art of conception' to use. He became a writer.

One of the last films Salim performed in was a black-and-white costume drama called *Sarhadi Lootera*. The director, S. M. Sagar, had been unable to find a dialogue writer, so he had handed the task to his clapper boy, Javed Akhtar.

Javed was the elder son of the leftist poet Jan Nissar Akhtar. When Javed was born, his father, a member of the Communist Party, had read the Communist Manifesto into his ear instead of the *Azaan*. His original

'Salim Khan and Javed Akhtar were a potent combination.'

name was Jadoo, taken from a line in a poem that Jan Nissar had written on the eve of his marriage: *'Lamha, lamha kisi jadoo ka fasana hoga.'* But when Jadoo was old enough for kindergarten, it was decided that he must have a proper name. The closest to Jadoo was Javed. The name Javed Akhtar means 'immortal star', but at that time few knew that the boy would live up to it.

In 1964, Javed came to the Mecca of Hindi cinema to meet the famous director Guru Dutt, but was unable to fulfil his ambition because five days after he arrived in Mumbai, Guru Dutt committed suicide. Javed stayed on in Mumbai, doing, for the first couple of years, whatever jobs he could find in the industry. It was around this time that S.M. Sagar offered him the job of a dialogue writer for his new film.

Sarhadi Lootera died a quick death at the box office, but Salim and Javed became friends. Both lived in Bandra. In the evenings, Javed would often go to Salim's house where they would cook up stories together.

Professionally, they weren't h..ving much luck. Salim had sold a story called *Do Bhai* to Brij Sadanah, and Javed had written the dialogue for another film, *Yakeen*. But both had flopped. They decided to team up. Among their first assignments together was developing a short story, *Adhikar*, for S. M. Sagar. They were paid Rs 5,000 each and their names didn't even feature on the credits. But Sagar's assistant, Sudhir Vahi, was impressed by *Adhikar* and suggested that the writers might try Sippy Films where a story department was being set up. The two presented themselves to G. P. Sippy and Ramesh at their newly acquired office in Khar for an interview. The duo narrated a story and suggested a few ideas. They were hired at Rs 750 a month each.

Salim Khan and Javed Akhtar were a potent combination. Salim's flamboyance, both in his personality and his writing style, was matched by Javed's easy confidence and eye for detail. They were witty and cocky and raring to go. Their inspiration came from Hollywood films, and they had little desire to be the typical *munimji* writers of Bollywood—anonymous men bent over pages for a pittance. Even before they had tasted success, Salim had predicted to writer Abrar Alvi that a day would come when writers would be paid as much as stars. A veteran of long years in the writing mills of Bollywood, Alvi had asked him: '*Dimaagh to kharab nahin hai?* (Have you taken leave of your senses?)'

The young writers flung themselves into the work at

the Sippy story department. They worked on *Andaaz* (with Gulzar) and then on *Seeta aur Geeta*. Salim-Javed wanted money and—more importantly—credit. They wanted to see their names on hoardings alongside those of the stars, and despite the success of *Seeta aur Geeta* they were angry with the Sippys because not only had they been excluded from the publicity, but the film, mostly written by them, had been credited to the Sippy story department. 'Heroes, directors, producers were the *zamindars* and writers were the scheduled caste,' says Salim. 'This position was not acceptable to us.'

The misunderstanding was sorted out in fifteen minutes. The duo met with Ramesh Sippy on the building terrace, and Ramesh promised them that in the next film they would have no cause to complain, it would be as much their film as his. In the then slow-changing world of Bollywood, this was an unprecedented development. In many ways it set the stage for a whole new movement in popular Hindi cinema.

*

The industry was ripe for change. The old guard—Raj Kapoor, Dev Anand, Dilip Kumar, Rajendra Kumar, Shammi Kapoor and Sunil Dutt—had passed on the baton to a new star, Rajesh Khanna. Rajesh was a phenomenon, India's first real super star who held a whole nation in thrall. But after a blaze of glory he seemed headed for burnout. The year 1972 started on a high note with *Dushman* and *Apna Desh*, but then the unthinkable happened: Rajesh delivered seven flops in a row. The crinkling eyes and the crooked smile did not seem to work their magic any more. The filmmakers too were at a loss. They had been routinely churning out the staple diet of romances and family socials because they worked so well at the box office. The names tell the tenor of the films: *Amar Prem, Daag, Aa Gale Lag Ja, Aradhana, Kati Patang, Aan Milo Sajna*. Now the old formulas were failing them.

The audience was growing restive. The saccharine on screen had little to do with their lives. The early seventies were a time of social and political upheaval. The post-Independence optimism of the fifties and sixties was slowly giving way to a deepening disillusionment with authority. The legacy of selflessness and integrity left by the politicians of the freedom struggle had been replaced with widespread corruption, and the use of violence for criminal and political ends was on the rise. The common citizen felt that law and order had broken down. The mood in the country was one of hopelessness and frustration, even anger, and a new morality was taking shape, typified by Jayaprakash Narayan's socialist movement. In a few months, Bachchan would give a face to this anger in *Zanjeer*.

Gopaldas Parmanand Sippy was the right man at the right time, he was a man who felt these changes in the air

and responded to them in his films. His mind was keen
and his instincts impeccable. He was a lawyer by training
and a gambler by nature. He had run a restaurant,
constructed buildings, produced films, directed films and
even dabbled in acting. G. P. had the knack for spotting
an opportunity, and the guts to run with it.

In 1947, the Sippys had migrated to Mumbai from
Karachi with only their shirts on their backs. Stories of
how G. P. built back the family fortune are now industry
folklore. Legend has it that he was eating in a restaurant
in Colaba when he noticed that there was a long line
outside the door. He asked his neighbour the reason and
was told that the offices in the area had just halted work
for lunch. G. P. decided to open a restaurant. He located
an appropriate shop, but he did not have the Rs 5000
required to rent it. In fact, he had hardly any money at all.
But in the morning he opened a bank account with Rs
100, and wrote out a cheque to the landlord. The shop
was his. G. P. then promptly mortgaged the shop for Rs
5000 and deposited the money in his bank.

There were always new interests to dabble in. At one
point, he had returning British Army soldiers carry
carpets to London for him. He would pay them a small
fee, collect the carpets in London and sell them for a
handsome profit. He also originated the idea of building
a co-operative society where flats could be sold
individually to owners. Until then, apartments were only
rented out. Mohini Mansion, Churchgate Mansion,

Anand Niwas and Gopal
Mansion are only a few of the
Mumbai buildings that stand
testimony to his unbeatable
chutzpah.

G. P. was seduced by
cinema while constructing a
home for Nargis. He kept
pestering her brother to make
a film for him. The film never
happened, but G. P. was
hooked for life. He started out
making B-grade crime thrillers
with names like *Black Cat, Mr
X, Lighthouse* and *Mr India*.
Then in 1965 began a gold run
that elevated him to A-list
status. The hits piled on
fast—*Mere Sanam, Johar-
Mehmood in Goa,
Brahmachari, Bandhan* and,
in 1971, Ramesh's *Andaaz*.

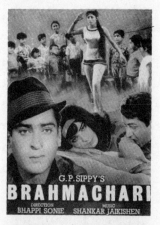

*'In 1965 began a gold run that
elevated G.P. Sippy to A-list status.'*

G. P. Sippy dreamed big.
After *Seeta aur Geeta*, he wasn't interested in repeating
the usual girl-boy romance. He wanted to make a
multi-starrer. There hadn't been a multi-starrer since Raj
Kapoor's *Mera Naam Joker* flopped in 1970 but G. P.
wasn't deterred. He was looking for scale and grandeur.

21

He asked his story department employees, Salim-Javed, to come up with something new.

Salim-Javed had been toying with a four-line idea for months. Producer Baldev Pushkarna had at first bought it for Rs 20,000, but his director, Manmohan Desai, to whom the duo narrated the idea in between shooting breaks at Worli, wasn't convinced. He asked them to develop *Chacha Bhatija*, a comedy, instead. Another producer, Prem Sethi, then bought the story idea for Prakash Mehra. But Mehra was too busy making *Zanjeer*. He released the idea at Salim-Javed's request. They then took it to the Sippys.

It was just the germ of a film: An army officer's family gets massacred. He remembers two junior officers who had been court-martialled. They are rascals but they are also brave. The retired officer decides to enlist them in his mission for revenge.

A meeting was scheduled at the Khar office. Salim-Javed narrated the idea to Ramesh and G. P. Sippy. In addition to the four lines, they also offered the Sippys a complete script called *Majboor*, about a man who, believing he has a brain tumour, agrees to be framed for a murder in return for money.

Ramesh was tempted by the script. It was ready to shoot. The film could be canned in less than a year. He could make *Majboor* while Salim-Javed developed the four-line idea. A discussion on money ensued: Salim-Javed wanted a lakh of rupees for developing the four lines and two lakhs for *Majboor*. Ramesh counter-offered: Rs 75,000 for developing the four lines and a lakh and a half for *Majboor*. Salim-Javed hesitated. Another producer had already offered more for the script, they would lose a lot of money in this deal. The Sippys didn't want that. They decided to let *Majboor* go. Besides, even Ramesh thought that while *Majboor* was a good script, it wasn't a great one. The meeting ended with G. P. Sippy saying decisively, 'I want to make a big film. Develop the four lines.'

CHAPTER 2

LOHA LOHE KO KAATATA HAI

It is an unlikely setting for history: a twelve-by-twelve room painted dreary beige, with dim yellow bulbs throwing light on an outsized semi-circular *diwan* and one barred window overlooking a terracotta-red boundary wall. *Sholay* was written here in a month.

The sessions started in March 1973. Every day, at around ten-thirty or eleven, Salim-Javed and Ramesh Sippy locked themselves into the Sippy Films writing room. Sprawled on the diwan, they wrestled with the plot. Four lines had to be developed into a three-hour film. Ideas were tossed back and forth, scenes written and rejected, characters created and killed. They argued and critiqued and helped each other plug the loopholes, consuming countless cups of strong, sweet *chai* to keep themselves alert. Sometimes the tea was replaced with beer. Sometimes G. P. Sippy dropped in.

Ramesh had bet his money on the four lines but he

wasn't happy with the backdrop. The logistics of making an army film were daunting. There were too many permissions to be sought and censorship could be a nightmare. '*Kuchh aur kar do* (Do something else),' he told his writers, and Salim-Javed changed the army man to a police officer. There were days when nothing came, and the three killed time with cigarettes and chat about Hollywood films. But this was rare. Mostly they just hurtled on. The characters kept coming through. It was as if the story was writing itself. 'There was a wave of creativity,' says Salim, 'like a sea at high tide.'

They wanted to create a big action adventure, an epic confrontation between good and evil. The inspiration was the Hollywood western. All three of them had been influenced greatly by films like *Butch Cassidy and the Sundance Kid*, *The Magnificent Seven*, Sergio Leone's spaghetti westerns, and, of course, the mother of the mercenary movie, Akira Kurosawa's *Seven Samurai*. They wanted to imitate the rugged feel of these films—the rough-hewn texture, the sprawling landscapes, the violence in close-up, the smell of horses and carriages. The idea was to do an Indian western.

As character graphs were plotted, symmetries fell into place without effort. The entire structure of the film is dominated by doublings, by symmetrical pairs of opposites. The prime mover of the story is a Thakur: principled, upright, spotlessly clean, with a clipped style of talking. His nemesis is a daku: amoral, sadistic, dirty

25

and gregarious. There are two friends: one, a flirtatious extrovert, and the other a sardonic introvert. There are two women: one, a colourful, uninhibited, jabbering *chhamakchhalo*, and the other a silent lady of the lamps in widow-white. And while there is never any doubt that the two heroes are the kind of friends who would gladly die for each other, unlike most Hindi movie pals they rarely express their affection for each other. In fact, they have nothing good to say about each other at all.

Salim-Javed found inspiration in the unlikeliest of places. The name Gabbar Singh was taken from a real-life dacoit. Salim remembered his father, a DIG in Indore, telling him about a dangerous dacoit who plundered villages around Gwalior in the '50s. His trademark was capturing cops and cutting off their noses and ears. Legend was that the real-life Gabbar was so against khaki uniforms that he once captured a postman and carved up his face, despite the man's desperate protests that he wasn't a policeman. Soorma Bhopali was someone Javed knew from his Bhopal days, and the barber Hariram Nai was a spillover from Salim's childhood—for five rupees he would give his father a shave and the children, haircuts. Veeru and Jai were the names of Salim's college friends. And Thakur Baldev Singh was his father-in-law. Singh, a Dogra from Jammu, was so against his daughter marrying a Muslim that he hadn't spoken to the couple for the first seven years of their marriage. All these names, these traits, found their way into the script.

26

A disgruntled parent also inspired the classic 'Veeru Ki Shaadi' proposal scene. Javed was in love with actress Honey Irani. They had first met on the sets of Seeta aur Geeta and much of their courtship was conducted there. But Mama Perin Irani kept a strict eye on her daughters. And Javed, still a struggling writer, had little to recommend him. He had presented himself but had failed to make any impression at all. Salim was a little senior. He had also worked in Bachpan, which Irani had produced. Naturally, Javed requested his partner to carry the proposal. He didn't know that the partner didn't approve either.

'A disgruntled parent also inspired the "Veeru ki Shaadi" scene.' Javed and Honey Irani on the sets of Seeta aur Geeta.

The exchange between Perin Irani and Salim went something like this:

'Ladka kaisa hai? (What's the boy like?)'

'We are partners and I wouldn't work with anyone unless I approve of him. Lekin daaru bahut peeta hai. (But he drinks too much.)'

'Kya? Daaru peeta hai! (What? Drinks too much!)'

'Aaj kal bahut nahin peeta hai, bas ek do peg. Aur ismein aisi koi kharabi nahin hai. Lekin daaru peene *ke baad red light area mein bhi jaata hai.* (Doesn't drink too much these days, only a peg or two. He's a decent sort, actually. Just that after he's had a bit to drink he does go down to the red light area.)'

Only the last line in the scene—*Khaandaan ka pata chalte hi aapko khabar kar denge* (As soon as we find out anything at all about his family we'll let you know)—is fiction.

Salim-Javed were not squeamish about pilfering, whether from life or the movies. The Hollywood western was the primary inspiration, but they looked closer home as well. Raj Khosla's 1971 hit, *Mera Gaon Mera Desh*, the story of a one-armed man who reforms a petty criminal and uses him to protect their village against dacoits, loomed like a ghost in the background. There was also Narendra Bedi's successful B-grade take on the western, *Khote Sikkey*, released the same year that *Sholay* was being written. The Bimal Roy classic, *Madhumati*, has a scene in which a boastful servant is caught by his master, much like what happens with Soorma Bhopali. And the coin motif—Jai tosses a coin before making any decision—came from a Gary Cooper starrer, *Garden of Evil*. But Salim-Javed weren't cheap imitators. Their genius lay in their ability to refashion ideas in ways more compelling than the original.

Fifteen days after Salim-Javed and Ramesh began their sessions in the dim-lit room, the outline for their new film was ready.

The location was the same—G. P. Sippy's terrace apartment—but this time the party was quieter. Only the principal cast and crew had been invited. Salim-Javed were there. The composer-lyricist team of R. D. Burman and Anand Bakshi, who had done *Seeta aur Geeta,* had been signed on again. But all eyes were on the stars who had made the cut—Dharmendra, Hema Malini, Amitabh Bachchan, Jaya Bhaduri, Sanjeev Kumar and Danny Dengzongpa.

The film had been conceived as a multi-starrer. But by the time the original idea had been developed into a full story outline, the list of characters had grown beyond what anyone had expected. Casting, naturally, had turned out to be a difficult process. Many names were discussed as the script developed. Dharmendra and Hema Malini were, of course, obvious choices after *Seeta aur Geeta*. In 1973, with five hits together, they were already established as a successful star pair.

Dharamendra, who had been delivering hits every year, had graduated from being Meena Kumari's boyfriend to a megastar. Raised in Sanewal, Punjab, Dhramendra grew up fascinated with films. As a little boy he often travelled miles to catch the touring cinema. He worked for some time for an American drilling company, but the lure of films was too great. He started his movie career in 1960 with Arjun Hingorani's *Dil Bhi*

Tera Hum Bhi Tere. The signing amount was fifty-one rupees and breakfast at a Grant Road restaurant. But he had come a very long way since. Besides, his impressive physique and easy smile made him perfect for the role of the flamboyant flirt, Veeru.

Hema Malini complemented Dharmendra in both looks and box office stature. *Seeta aur Geeta* had won her the best actress Filmfare Award and the number one position in Bollywood. Incredibly enough, in 1964 her first director, Sridhar, had thrown her out of a Tamil film, declaring that she had no star appeal. The rejection had only strengthened Hema's resolve. When her debut Hindi film, *Sapnon Ka Saudagar,* was released, giant posters carried her picture with the line: 'Watch the Dreamgirl seduce Raj Kapoor.' The tag proved prophetic: Hema did become the Dreamgirl of the masses, especially after she hit big time with the 1970 golden jubilee film *Johnny Mera Naam.*

But Hema wasn't too keen to play the *tangewali.* She had been the backbone of both *Andaaz* and *Seeta aur Geeta* and Basanti's five and a half scenes seemed too small. 'Why like this?' she asked Ramesh. '*Yeh kya hai?* (What is this?)' Ramesh was frank. 'This isn't your film,' he said, '*yeh Sanjeev aur Gabbar ki film hai* (This is Sanjeev's and Gabbar's film). But your role will be very interesting.' Another director might have had to look elsewhere but Ramesh had helped create the Hema stardom. She knew he could work wonders. At Ramesh's insistence, Hema agreed.

The big question was, who would play the second male lead, Jai? Shatrughan Sinha, cocky and flamboyant, was hot, a villain with a fan following to rival that of the heroes'. The distributors, too, were keen on him. But Salim-Javed were sold on Amitabh. Perhaps the only people in all of India to have thrice watched his colossal dud, *Raaste ka Pathar*, the writers were convinced that Amitabh was an exceptional artiste. The older son of noted Hindi poet Harivanshrai Bachchan, Amitabh had given up a job as a freight broker for the shipping firm Bird & Company in Calcutta to pursue an acting career. But he wasn't having much luck. His distinctive voice was rejected by All India Radio, and in his early film, *Reshma aur Shera*, he had played a mute. As his films continued to flop, roles became scarce. In *Duniya ka Mela*, he was replaced by Sanjay Khan. But Salim-Javed, who had already convinced Prakash Mehra to cast him in *Zanjeer*, kept the faith.

Ramesh toyed with the idea of signing on Shatru but finally decided that he was too big a star. Three mega-watt stars translate into mega-watt ego problems. Ramesh had seen both *Bombay to Goa* and *Anand*, and was impressed by Amitabh's talent. Meanwhile, Amitabh had also asked Dharmendra to put in a word. The lobbying worked. Amitabh was cast as Jai.

Pran was a strong contender for the Thakur's role. Once a leading villain in Hindi films, he had become a

character actor with a big draw. He had also worked in
earlier Sippy productions like *Mere Sanam* and
Brahmachari. But Ramesh decided that Sanjeev Kumar
was a better choice. In *Seeta aur Geeta*, Sanjeev had
played the generic hero role, but his acting prowess had
already been established with films like *Khilona, Koshish*
and *Parichay*. Born into a traditional Gujarati family,

Sanjeev came to films via the
theatre. He worked with the
Indian People's Theatre
Association (IPTA), mostly
playing the role of an old
man. He didn't like that. He
was a thirty-year-old playing
seventy-year-old characters.
One day he asked IPTA
veteran, A. K. Hangal, why he
was never cast as the hero.
'*Hero ke role main kya
rakkha hai?* (What's so

*'Ramesh toyed with the idea of sign-
ing on Shatru but he was too big a
star . . . Amitabh was cast as Jai.'*

special about a hero's role?)' Hangal had replied. '*Agar
shuru main tumhein hero ka role diya to hero hi bana
rahega. Actor kabhi nahin banega.* (If you start with a
hero's role, that's all you'll remain. You'll never become
an actor.)' And Sanjeev was, foremost, an actor.

As was Jaya Bhaduri. The diminutive actress, who had
started her career with a small role in Satyajit Ray's
Mahanagar, had become a big star with *Guddi*. The

32

widow's role that she was being offered in the new film wasn't much on paper. The footage was less than Hema's. It was, literally, less colourful. But who else, asks Ramesh, 'could convey through her eyes, facial expressions and body language, the kind of feelings that Jaya could? There wasn't another actress of that calibre at the time.' Jaya wasn't so sure. She wondered if she should do such a small role. But she was seeing Amitabh at the time. Their first two films together, *Ek Nazar* and *Bansi Birju*, had flopped but two more, *Zanjeer* and *Abhimaan*, were due for release. 'Everything is nice,' Amitabh told her, 'we'll be together, it's a nice film, nice set-up. It suits you.' She agreed.

For the important role of the dacoit, Ramesh zeroed in on Danny Dengzongpa. The Film and Television Institute of India (FTII) graduate had become an in-demand villain after playing the wheelchair-bound psychotic husband in *Dhund*. Javed wasn't too excited about the choice, but Danny had both exotic looks and acting talent.

With dialogue, the characters started to breathe. As the skeletal sketches were fleshed out, the script gained new dimensions. The dialogue was first discussed and then written. Putting pen to paper was Javed's job, but his script was mostly illegible. He wrote furiously in Urdu, often at his bandstand house, while an assistant, Khalish, waited. Javed wrote entire scenes at a time, without crossing out or rethinking. The script was then written out in Hindi by Khalish while another assistant,

Amarjeet, typed out the one-line summary in English.

With each line, Gabbar Singh grew in stature. He wasn't the run-of-the-mill daku but a larger-than-life bandit on the lines of Sergio Leone's villains. He belonged to a place, as Javed says, 'somewhere between Mexico and Uttar Pradesh'. His character was unpredictable and his language familiar but eccentric. Gabbar had his own dialect—a *Ganga Jamuna*-inspired mix of Khadi Boli with a flavour of Avadhi. There was a peculiar coarseness in his lines, a sadism even in his choice of words, and it was this undiluted, earthy violence that would eventually have millions of Indians repeating his lines and even shelling out hard-earned rupees to buy records of the film's dialogue.

Sambha, the bit role that would immortalize character actor Macmohan, was factored in only as the dialogue was being written. The writers wanted to say that Gabbar Singh had a Rs 50,000 reward on his head. But they thought that a man of Gabbar's arrogance would probably order a flunkie to boast for him. So the following lines were written:

'*Arre o Sambha, kitna inaam rakhe hain sarkaar hum par?* (Sambha, what's the reward the government's fixed for my head?)'
'*Poore pachaas hazaar.* (A full fifty thousand.)'
'*Suna? Poore pachaas hazaar.* (Hear that? A full fifty thousand.)'

34

Sambha, Gabbar's echo, was then integrated into the screenplay.

Gabbar's language was so powerful that when the dialogue version was narrated to Amitabh, he wanted to play Gabbar. Salim-Javed were perhaps the only writers at the time who gave complete narrations, down to the ambience and last cut. The narration would be perfect teamwork, with Javed talking and Salim stressing a point in places, or interspersing with more detail. Hearing them narrate was like watching the film, frame by frame. Amitabh was convinced that Gabbar's was the better role. So was Sanjeev Kumar.

When Sanjeev first heard the script, he was shocked by the violence. 'When we reached interval point,' says Javed, 'his face was crushed. It was like somebody punches you on the nose. Sanjeev was totally taken aback.' Sanjeev had agreed to do the film, but after hearing the dialogue, he wanted Danny's role. The character fascinated him. But he didn't insist for long. Because ultimately Gabbar was a villain, and the violence disturbed Sanjeev. And no matter how colourful Ravan is, the victor is always Ram.

In fact the script shaped up so well that every actor was tempted by the others' roles. Dharmendra heard the final script enthralled like a child. And then asked if he could play the Thakur. The actor in him instinctively knew that he may be the hero but finally it was the Thakur's story. He was the prime mover. 'We can talk about it if you want,' Ramesh said, 'but don't forget that even though he is central, it is a character role. Besides, if we switch roles, then Sanjeev gets Hema Malini in the end.' The Dharmendra-Hema romance had just begun, and Sanjeev had already proposed to Hema once. Dharmendra gave Ramesh a look and made a quick decision. 'Veeru is good. I think I'll stick to playing Veeru.'

*

The team had one mantra: No Compromise. Ramesh was a methodical and organized man. Even the peripheral characters were fleshed out in detail. Asrani, a popular comedian of the time, was called in for the jailer's role. While Javed narrated, Salim explained the characterization: this man was an eccentric jailer, a

'The Dharmendra -Hema romance had just begun, and Sanjeev had already proposed to Hema once.'

blow-hard man, hollow from the inside. Asrani agreed, wondering whether he would be able to deliver the goods.

At a second meeting, Javed brought a World War II book, which had several pictures of Hitler posing. The jailer's get-up would be Hitler-inspired, much like Chaplin in *The Great Dictator*. Akhtar bhai from Kachin's made the outfit and Kabir the wig maker was brought in to fix the hair-do. '*Itne chhote se role ke liye itna detail,*' Asrani says, '*yeh log to kamaal kar rahe the.* (Such detail for so small a role—these people were excelling themselves.)' The jailer's lines were perfected by Asrani himself. As a student of FTII, he remembered a teacher talking about recordings of Hitler's speeches. He would start at a high pitch and only go higher. It was the perfect ploy to stir passions. To this Asrani added Jack Lemmon's 'Ha Ha' from a film called *The Great Race*.

The character of Soorma Bhopali had been gestating for years. Finding the right actor here proved easy. Actor Jagdeep had been starring in Sippy productions since he was a nine-year-old child. In *Sazaa*, he played a *banjara* boy singing '*tonguli, tonguli*'. In *Shahenshah*, he was the little guy fanning the heroine Kamini Kaushal. But it was *Brahmachari* that had given him his break as a comedian. Jagdeep had never been to Bhopal, Soorma's hometown. But while working in *Sarhadi Lootera*, he had met Javed, and they had hit it off well. Both were excellent mimics. One evening, during a post-shoot mimicry session, Javed imitated the way some women speak in Bhopal. Jagdeep picked it up and it became a running joke between them. Years later, when Salim-Javed were crafting the screenplay, Javed remembered Jagdeep.

One by one things fell into place. The film was named *Sholay*, spelt with an A and a Y instead of an E. In 1953, B. R. Chopra had made a film with the same name spelt as *Shole*. Javed had seen it as a child. G. P. Sippy had distributed it in Mumbai. *Shole* seemed puny. But *Sholay* evoked a sense of grandeur and high-octane action.

Perhaps, as Salim says, the stars were in the right configuration. Around then, Ramesh won a twelve-lakh-rupee jackpot at the races. And G. P. Sippy made another momentous decision: the dakus would not pillage villages in dhoti and *tikka*. *Sholay* was going to be a 'modern' film. Until then, all Hindi film dacoits came from the same cookie-cutter: they worshipped 'Ma Bhavani', wore dhotis and big *pagdis,* had four-inch tikkas on their foreheads, and roamed dusty valleys that were usually Rajasthan posing as Chambal. They were bad but honourable. In the landmark dacoit film *Ganga Jamuna*, Dilip Kumar became a dacoit after being framed for a crime. In the midst of murder, he retained his goodness. As did Sunil Dutt in *Mujhe Jeene Do*. Even Vinod Khanna in *Mera Gaon Mera Desh* was a noble savage; his cruelty had ethics. The Sippys wanted none of these easy cliches. Gabbar was amoral. He was the distilled essence of evil. He could never be reformed because he had no sense of right or wrong. And he wore army fatigues.

The original main cast for Sholay *with Ramesh and G.P. Sippy:*
Danny, Dharmendra, Hema, Sanjeev, Jaya and Amitabh.

Veeru and Jai were to be denim-clad city slickers. For
the shoot, Amitabh took along his favourite pair of jeans
and a jean jacket covered with '60s-style stickers popular
at the time. Ramesh removed the stickers and the jeans
stayed. Danny too had his own ideas for Gabbar. Perhaps
Gabbar could have long hair and a moustache and a
poncho, like Sergio Leone's baddies.

In May 1973, a full-page spread appeared in *Screen*.
Sanjeev, Dharmendra, Hema, Amitabh, Jaya and Danny
stared out of the page. A fire loomed in the background.
Sholay was coming.

CHAPTER 3

KEEMAT JO TUM CHAAHO, KAAM JO MEIN CHAAHUN

Ramesh didn't want ravines. The Sippys had decided to do away with the traditional daku dress, the dhoti, and now they also wanted to get rid of the traditional daku domain, the Chambal valley. Instead of the familiar dusty inclines, Ramesh visualized a harsher, more remote location. He wanted a place cut off from civilization, a village that time forgot. *Sholay* had to look different from all the dacoit films that had gone before. Ramesh summoned art director Ram Yedekar.

Yedekar was a pint-sized powerhouse. An uncompromising, no-nonsense man who spoke English in crisp, clipped sentences, he had little patience for the vagaries of the Hindi film industry. He worked exclusively on foreign film projects and only occasionally took on the odd Hindi film. He had done the art direction for Dev Anand's *Guide* and for the 1971 smash hit *Mera*

Gaon Mera Desh, Raj Khosla's reformed criminal-versus-dacoits story that was one of the original inspirations for *Sholay*. When the call came from Sippy productions, Yedekar didn't exactly jump at the offer. Instead he asked, 'Why me?' Ramesh replied, 'Because you've done *Mera Gaon Mera Desh*.'

Like Ramesh, Yedekar wasn't keen on returning to Rajasthan, the industry's favourite Chambal substitute. 'A hundred dacoit films have already been done there,' he said. He asked for a synopsis and a brief. The next day, he was given an outline. One of the requirements was a topography that allowed the Thakur's house to overlook the village. The art director pondered and suggested scouting the South. He wanted a month, and by the end of that period Ramesh would have his location. It was an unconventional suggestion; no dacoit movie had been shot in the South before. But that was the allure. The unprecedented visuals would set the film apart from the rest of the genre. Ramesh liked the idea.

Yedekar headed South in his car, a filmi Christopher Columbus in search of new vistas. He took only his driver and his cook with him. Driving hundreds of miles, they combed the areas around Mangalore, Bangalore and Cochin. When fatigue overtook them, they just stopped wherever they were, cooked by the side of the road and slept inside the car. Yedekar shot hundreds of photographs, searching for something that would match the frames in Ramesh's mind. The up-down geography

41

that was required presented the real challenge: Yedekar couldn't find a space that would encompass both the Thakur's house on a hill and a village spread out below.

One day, driving around in the vicinity of Bangalore, Yedekar remembered a location not far from the city where he had shot an English film called *Maya* some years ago. He asked his driver to head for the same hilly region. At around four in the afternoon, they arrived at Ramanagaram. Yedekar enquired of the locals, '*Yehi hai pahadi jahan angrezi film bani thi?* (Is this the hill where the English film was made?)' They confirmed the location. The road ahead narrowed into a small path and then disappeared into just brush. The car couldn't make it. So Yedekar walked the next few kilometers. He spent a couple of hours at the spot. That evening he returned to Bangalore and called Ramesh. There were two options, he said. One was a location near the Tumkur area on the Bangalore-Mumbai highway. The other was Ramanagaram.

*

Ramanagaram, an hour's drive from Bangalore, has a varied topography. Building-sized black boulders arch toward the sky. Small knolls segue into grassy flatlands. It is austere but textured. Ramesh loved it. He flew in the next day with his cinematographer, Dwarka Divecha, and two assistants from the production and direction departments. 'It captured my imagination,' he says. 'I was fascinated.' Divecha cast his eagle eye on the landscape, and confirmed the decision.

Pleasing Divecha wasn't easy. He was a crotchety old curmudgeon with a painter's eye and a sailor's mouth. He could be extremely difficult, but if you wanted the best for your film, you put up with it.

'Pleasing Divecha wasn't easy . . .
His reputation was fierce.'

He had experienced the ugliness of life, and he hadn't survived by being soft. His father had died when he was just a child, and then it was his widowed mother who'd had to bring up the children alone. The family was horribly poor, and there was rarely enough to eat. It was the boy's extraordinary strength of character that had seen him through those years. A fourth-standard dropout, Divecha was a self-taught man. Even as a little boy, he would walk to a nearby pavement bookstall and pay the vendor a few paise to let him stand there and read books.

Divecha had started his film career in 1936 as an assistant cameraman and gradually worked his way up. Top directors like Kardar, H. S. Rawail and L. V. Prasad all swore by him. His reputation was fierce. Dressed in a white bosky bush shirt, white pants and black shoes,

43

Divecha saab was a Hitler on the sets. A stickler for punctuality, he would let loose on assistants even if they were late by a minute: '*Aadmi ho ya janwar*,' he would scream, '*tumko timing samajh nahin aati kya?* (Are you a bloody animal! Can't you understand the concept of time?)' If he happened to arrive at a set early, he would wait in the car and walk into the set only at the exact minute the shift was scheduled to start. But the temper wasn't reserved for underlings alone. Even top stars rarely escaped Divecha's wrath. He made the stars stand in place while he lit shots—substitutes weren't allowed—and shouted if they fidgeted: '*Hema, itna kyun hilti hai?* (Why do you move so much, Hema?)'

But off the set, Hitler thawed into a colourful, affectionate man. He was a *shaukeen aadmi*, with a taste for the good things in life. When he wasn't shooting, Divecha would be at home, ensconced in his favourite chair, holding a glass (always whisky) and a cigarette (Chesterfield or Camel), either listening to music (ghazals) or reading a book. He had a large collection of Popular Mechanics magazines and technical books. When he spoke, he might have been a scholar, except that he swore incessantly. Divecha had no children but kept a large Alsatian dog, whom he called his son. He could be frustratingly rigid but was also a sucker for a love story. Industry folklore had it that Divecha was instrumental in the legendary Dev Anand-Suraiya romance. The only man allowed into Suraiya's house, he often carried Dev

'Ramanagaram was a vast emptiness . . . waiting to be fashioned into fantasy.'

Anand's love letters to her.

Like Ramesh, Divecha was a rigorous perfectionist. Ramanagaram was a vast emptiness; for the young director and the fastidious cinematographer it was a blank canvas waiting to be fashioned into fantasy. But for the producer, Sippy senior, for whom infrastructure was critical, it was a nightmare. There was nothing there other than a few fields and some huts. The entire village had to be constructed, starting with a road leading up to the location. Within weeks of Ramesh's approval, an army descended upon Ramanagaram. Permissions were sought from the farmers around the area and then the

45

work began. A crew of nearly a hundred people—thirty from Mumbai and sixty to seventy locals—worked round the clock. In places the ground had to be levelled, and in others steps had to be cut into the hard earth. The sets, from the Thakur's house to Gabbar's den, had to be within walking distance of one another. The script also required a temple and a mosque.

But the sets had to do more than just look realistic. They also had to support a gigantic film crew through long hours of shooting, from scythes to spot-boys to stars. The logistics were daunting. It was up to the construction manager to tackle this gargantuan problem, and Ramesh had found the best man for the job: Aziz Hanif Sheikh. Aziz bhai, who had been working since the actress Suraiya's time, was a sprightly old man with an ingenious mind. He had never met a problem he couldn't solve. He made huts collapse, built gadgets, constructed roads and levelled thigh-high vegetation overnight.

Aziz planned meticulously. Gabbar's den was made just behind the Thakur's house. Make-up rooms with attached bathrooms were cleverly constructed inside the villagers' houses and a sophisticated drainage system was laid out. There was a godown to store rations and a kitchen equipped to feed a thousand people. There were barns where the horses would be lodged and rooms where the construction crew could stay permanently. A road that led from the Bangalore highway to Ramanagaram was built. Telephone lines were installed.

And all this was done in two months.

*

While the workers toiled in the Bangalore sun, Ramesh sweated it out in Mumbai. The music sittings had started. R. D. Burman was at his peak in the early '70s. He had created a slew of outstanding songs—most of them sung by Kishore Kumar—in films such as *Kati Patang*, *Amar Prem* and *Namak Haram*. There were rumours that even *Aradhana*'s rollicking '*Mere sapnon ki rani*', though credited to his father, the legendary S. D. Burman, was actually an R. D. creation. Rahul's genius lay in his astounding versatility—in 1971 he had composed both *Hare Rama, Hare Krishna*'s rocking '*Dum maro dum*', which plays in discos even today, and *Amar Prem*'s classical-based '*Raina beeti jaaye*'. It was said that S. D. had nicknamed him Pancham because even as a child he would cry in all five notes. But Rahul wasn't one for rules. Even in his classical compositions he wouldn't restrict himself to the grammar. His motto was: 'What sounds good to the ears is grammar.'

Pancham *da* held sittings with Ramesh in his Odena building apartment in Khar. Ramesh would often be joined by Salim-Javed and sometimes by the dance director, P. L. Raj, and G. P. Sippy. Pancham's way of functioning was this: He would tell his directors to narrate the story in a nutshell but to describe the song

47

situations in elaborate detail. An assistant would make copious notes during the narration. Sometimes, after the narration Pancham would pull out ten appropriate tunes from his bank. The ten would be narrowed to five, which he would polish and present to the director at the next sitting. Or he might reject them all and start afresh. Javed narrated *Sholay* to Pancham. Ramesh had specific ideas about song situations and it was his habit to discuss everything. Despite this, two sittings were usually enough for creating the actual song. '*Koi haseena jab rooth jaati hai*' was the first song composed.

'*R.D. Burman was at his peak in the early seventies.*'

For most songs that Pancham created, the tunes were composed first and then the lyrics were written. For *Sholay* Anand Bakshi penned the lyrics at an astonishing speed. Like Pancham, Bakshi was also at his creative peak. An army man turned songster, he was the king of lyrics in the '70s. Of the star lyricists who were his immediate predecessors, Shailendra was dead and Sahir Ludhianvi had aged into a temperamental artist. Sahir was a favourite of G.P. Sippy's: G.P. had first tasted alcohol at Sahir's insistence that the producer could never understand his lyrics—*Mujhko na koi hosh na gham, main nashe main hoon,* from the movie *Marine Drive*—if he did not drink. But Bakshi was hitting the high notes with successes like *Amar Prem.* Besides, he had already notched up a winner in *Seeta aur Geeta.* He couldn't match Sahir's refined aesthetics, but he was exceptionally proficient and speedy— some of the songs were written in just half an hour—and that had its own merits. Also, *Sholay* had nothing in common with the sensitive, emotion-driven musicals and love stories of the '60s in which Sahir's songs had worked their magic.

Most of the songs for *Sholay* were recorded at Rajkamal studios. Multi-tracking hadn't arrived yet, and at the time Rajkamal was the only studio with a six-track system. Singers sometimes had the liberty of dubbing separately, but the full orchestra had to play together—sixty or seventy musicians, all necessarily playing perfectly, because one note out of place meant starting all over again. First Pancham's assistants, Manori and Basu, would put the finishing touches in place, complete the technical work and do rehearsals. Then Pancham would come on to do the final balancing of sounds. The string section and the rhythm section sat in the main Rajkamal hall, but the brass section, with its trumpets and trombones, kept spilling over from its assigned area into the other microphones. So the trumpet and trombone players were shifted to the adjoining preview theatre. Among the musicians were two outstanding players, who sat at the santoor and flute: Shivkumar Sharma and Hariprasad Chaurasia.

Soorma Bhopali would get to sing a song: there was room, the writers decided, for a *qawwali* in the comedy track of the film. But Javed suggested the *chaar bhaand* of Bhopal instead of a qawwali. Chaar bhaand, a dying art, is a composition sung by four groups, instead of the qawwali's traditional two, with the audience enjoying the exchange sitting in the middle of all four. Through Javed's contacts, a chaar bhaand group was found in Bhopal. They came to Mumbai and played for Pancham in his music room. He developed a qawwali along chaar bhaand lines—an eight-minute-long musical interplay of words and wit between four singers. The lyrics:

Chaand sa koi chehra na pehloo main ho
To chandni ka mazaa nahin aata.

Jaam peekar sharaabi na gir jaaye to
Maikashi ka mazaa nahin aata
(There is no joy in moonlight
Without the moon-faced one by my side.
There is no joy in wine
If having drunk I do not stumble and fall.)

The singers were Kishore Kumar, Manna Dey, Bhupinder and Anand Bakshi himself. The qawwali was recorded but never shot—the film was already longer than the requisite three hours. Bakshi was the most disheartened. 'Perhaps if they had kept it,' he wonders, 'I might have had a career as a singer.'

The music had been sold to Polydor for an advance royalty of five lakh rupees. Because the sixth song, the qawwali, didn't make it to the final soundtrack, the deal worked out to one lakh rupees per song. It was the biggest deal at the time. In the early '70s music did not translate into money. There was one company, HMV, and one medium, the vinyl record. Producers gratefully sold music rights for a pittance. Within such a total monopoly, HMV's word was law. A record cost as much as fifty rupees, and gramophones were passed down from generation to generation. Naturally, then, the market was small. In fact, when Polydor entered the market in 1970, the entire music market was valued at three crores of rupees, less than half of what the music from one A-list banner film might sell for now.

The system of advance royalty that Polydor started with Sholay was the first deal of its kind in India. The Sippys and Polydor had more than just a business relationship—Ramesh was married to Geeta, the sister of Polydor owner Shashi Patel. Polydor was keen to work out the best deal. A five-lakh-rupee payment was a show of great confidence; to recover the money Polydor would need to sell 100,000 records in such a top-end market where 25,000 units was considered a good sale.

*

Danny had been signing films indiscriminately after *Dhund*. Fighting sniggers and racist remarks, the Sikkimese actor had become a star, and he wasn't going to let the opportunity go. One of the films he had signed was Feroz Khan's *Dharmatma*, a *desi* version of Francis Ford Coppola's classic, *The Godfather*. *Dharmatma* was to be shot extensively in Afghanistan. Months had been spent on clearing the bureaucratic maze and getting the necessary permissions. All the logistics were in place and shooting was to begin in October. Then the dates for *Sholay* were finalized, also for October.

Danny wanted to do both films. They were both big-banner projects with meaty roles. His secretary Madan Arora was instructed to find a solution. Madan asked Feroz Khan to shift his schedule. But with so many bureaucratic hurdles, it would be impossible to reschedule dates. Feroz refused. Madan then approached Ramesh. But the Sippys had already got combination dates from the other stars—Sanjeev, Amitabh, Hema and Jaya. Shifting schedules would have meant re-juggling everyone's date diary. It was equally impossible. Feroz couldn't even give a confirmation on when Danny would return from Afghanistan. Bad weather, bad acting, anything could cause a delay. They had to factor in a few extra days just to be sure.

Madan, Feroz and Ramesh locked heads over the mess. But they couldn't find a satisfactory solution. Feroz wouldn't budge. And he was angry with Danny over the last-minute confusion. They were friends and co-stars and the commitment had been made before *Sholay*. Danny could hardly back out of it now as Feroz was gearing up to go on his outdoor shoot. The tension continued for a fortnight. Then Danny made his decision. He knew that *Sholay* was the bigger film, but he couldn't let Feroz down. Danny said no to Gabbar.

CHAPTER 4

MUJHE GABBAR CHAAHIYE—ZINDA

Amjad Khan filled the doorway. He was not a particularly large man, but his lumbering gait, thickset face and curly hair gave him the appearance of one. Ramesh was lying on the diwan with his back to the door. He craned his head right and up for a look. From the low angle, Amjad loomed larger. Something clicked. 'He had an interesting face,' says Ramesh. 'I felt very positive.'

Panic had set in after Danny's departure. Shooting was less than a month away. And Gabbar Singh was no ordinary character. It was a pivotal role. The actor had to have both talent and charisma to hold his own against the galaxy of stars. Bad casting could destroy the film. The Sippys considered the villains of the day—Ranjit, Prem Chopra—but none fit the bill. In desperation, they even toyed with the idea of casting Premnath, clearly past his prime, as Gabbar. But he had bloated too much physically and had a reputation for being difficult. There were already enough star egos to handle on this film. In the anxious discussions, Amjad Khan's name came up.

Amjad was the younger son of character artiste Jayant. In the world of movies, he was just another struggling actor. His home production, *Patthar ke Sanam*, which was supposed to launch him as a hero, was announced but never made. He had assisted K. Asif in *Love and God* and also done a bit role in the film. The credentials were hardly impressive. But in the arena of theatre Amjad had a strong reputation. Javed had first seen him perform in 1963 at the annual youth festival held at the Tal Katora gardens in Delhi. Amjad had played the part of an army officer in a play called *Ae Mere Watan ke Logon*. Ramesh saw him years later on the Mumbai stage, in a play called *To This Night A Dawn*, in which Ramesh's sister, Soni, was playing Amjad's mother. But it was Salim who remembered the young actor's name.

A few days after Danny left, Salim bumped into Amjad at the Bandra bandstand. Salim knew Amjad's father, and had been visiting their home since Amjad was a little boy. A polite conversation ensued in which Salim asked Amjad about work. There wasn't much, just bit roles and theatre. Salim had heard about Amjad's skills as an actor, and physically he seemed to fit the role. 'I can't promise you anything,' he told Amjad, 'but there is a role in a big film. I'll take you to the director. *Agar aapko yeh role mil jaaye, aapki koshish se ya aapki kismat se* (If you get this role, whether by luck or effort), I tell you, it is the finest role in this film.'

Amjad seemed to fit the part, but he was unknown. Could he carry the film? He was asked to grow a beard and come back. Meanwhile Ramesh and Salim-Javed pondered. Salim-Javed were convinced that Amjad was the right choice. One day, actor Satyen Kappu happened to be in the office. Kappu, who did theatre with IPTA, had been signed on for the role of the Thakur's servant, Ramlal. Out of the blue, Salim asked him: '*Kappu saab, kya Amjad aapse achha artiste hai?* (Kappu sahib, is Amjad a better artiste than you?)' Kappu immediately said: '*Haan, mujhse achha actor hai, young hai, uski thinking fresh hai.* (Yes he is. He's young and his thinking is fresh.)'

'*Amjad seemed to fit the part, but he was unknown. Could he carry the film?*'

Four days later, a screen test was done. They shot pictures in the office garden. Amjad had grown a beard and blackened his teeth. His diction was right, his language was perfect. He was confirmed for the role. Amjad hurried ecstatically to the hospital to break the news to his wife Shaila. The date was 20 September 1973. His son Shadaab was born at ten minutes past four that afternoon.

*

Sholay grew from paper into plans, and it gained weight and size and ambition. The Sippys wanted to make *Sholay* the biggest and the best adventure film ever, and they would make no compromises. The traditional 35mm format, they felt, wouldn't do justice to their vision. They were aiming for epic grandeur. So a decision was made: *Sholay* would be India's first 70mm film with stereophonic sound.

The 70mm film format offered double the size. The major Hollywood action movies at the time, such as *McKenna's Gold*, were shot in this format because it gave the viewer, quite literally, a big movie experience. But the decision to do *Sholay* in this format added another layer of complications. Shooting in 70mm wasn't easy. It required huge cameras which could take 70mm film. Importing these cameras was an expensive proposition. The most practical solution was to shoot on 35mm and then blow it up for 70mm.

The format was screen-tested. Divecha suggested putting a ground glass in front of the camera lens, on which Kamlakar Rao, a young but technically skilled cameraman, made markings so the margins of the 70mm frame could be identified. Ramesh's brother Ajit, who lived in London, forwarded the test to Paris, where a 70mm print was made. The print came back with further

SHOLAY

instructions on how to perfect the technique. A 70mm film also required bigger screens, and most theatres in India weren't equipped for it. The Sippys decided to have two sets of negatives, one in 70mm and the other in 35mm. In practical terms, this meant that every shot would have to be done twice.

Each decision added to the cost. The Sippy's were planning a one-crore film. The budget couldn't exceed that because the film was already selling at an exorbitant price. The Rajshris, who had been distributing Sippy films since *Adl-e-Jehangir*, had bought the film at Rs 22.5 lakh per territory, double the going price at the time. Tarachand Barjatya, the grand patriarch of the family, was confident of recovering his price. He bought *Sholay* for Delhi-U.P, Punjab and Nizam. In a few territories—Rajasthan, the Central Provinces, Tamil Nadu and Kerala—the Rajshris were to release the film on behalf of the Sippys. In the Bombay territory, the Sippys would distribute themselves.

While Ramesh and Divecha worked hard at perfecting camera technique, Amitabh and Jaya got married. And Prakash Mehra's *Zanjeer* was released in May. Amitabh and Jaya had been seeing each other for a few years. Their earlier screen pairings had been disasters, but the couple had promised themselves that if Prakash Mehra's revenge saga worked, they would take a holiday trip to London. *Zanjeer* hit home like a slap on the face. Its spare look and vigilante politics embodied the country's zeitgeist.

58

like no other film of the time. It set the course for Hindi cinema, and made Amitabh a huge star.

But even stars didn't take holidays with their girlfriends without first marrying. London would be Amitabh's first trip abroad and he was very excited, but his more conservative parents drew the line. 'You must marry,' Harivansh Rai and Teji Bachchan said. The couple's response was immediate: 'Okay, we'll marry tomorrow.' Jaya was already part of *Sholay*, and Amitabh wondered whether the marriage would affect the casting. He checked with Ramesh. Ramesh assured him that the marriage wouldn't change anything. They would go ahead with the original plan for the film. 'Fine,' Amitabh said, 'then I'm going on a honeymoon.'

Amitabh and Jaya were married on 3 June 1973. During the ceremony they were slipping the pundit 100-rupee notes, egging him on to hurry through the ceremony because they were afraid that they would miss the flight to London.

When they returned from London, Ramesh had another problem to deal with—Jaya, playing the quiet, self-denying widow,

'While Ramesh and Divecha worked on camera technique, Amitabh and Jaya got married. And Zanjeer was released in May.'

59

had come back from her honeymoon pregnant.

*

Amjad prepared for Gabbar. Normal life took a back seat; this was clearly the best role of his career. Amjad devoured *Abhishapth Chambal*, a book on Chambal dacoits written by Jaya Bhaduri's father, Taroon Coomar. He marked out the pages on the real-life Gabbar, insisting that Shaila read it too. He rehearsed his lines and fleshed out his character. He remembered a *dhobi* from his childhood days who used to call out to his wife: '*Arre o Shanti*.' The lilt in Gabbar's '*Arre o Sambha*' came from this dhobi.

Amjad was enthusiastic but insecure, and badgered his wife constantly:

'Do you think I'll be able to do it?'

'Of course,' she would say, 'you're a good actor. I've seen all your plays.'

'But this is a different ball game.'

'So what? You've been part of *Love and God* . . . your father is an actor . . . '

'All that doesn't matter. Do you think I'll be able to do this?'

The morning Amjad was to leave for Bangalore, he put the Quran on his head and prayed. Shaila was surprised. Amjad was a spiritual person but he rarely prayed. As abruptly as he had started, he stopped. He placed the holy book back in its place, said, 'I think I'll be able to do it,' and drove to the airport.

The flight didn't reach Bangalore. There was a hydraulic failure, and the pilot was forced to keep circling over Mumbai. After dumping fuel for hours, the plane landed back in Mumbai. Amjad sat at the airport but didn't call home. After five hours, it was announced that the technical faults had been fixed and the plane was ready for take-off. Not many passengers had the stomach to get on that plane again. Amjad was among the four or five who finally flew on it. He *had* to reach Bangalore. Through the flight, he wasn't thinking about his wife or his one-month-old son. His only terror was: 'If this plane crashes, Danny gets Gabbar.'

CHAPTER 5

LOHA GARAM HAI—MAAR DO HATHODA

The second day of October, 1973. The rain was coming down in sheets. The pellet-hard drops turned roads into slush and daylight into dusk. There was no way the generator and camera would make it up the hill to the Thakur's house.

Ramesh had woken up that morning with the peculiar adrenalin rush that the first day of shooting brings. He was a walking whirlwind of contradictory emotions: he was excited, anxious, ambitious, jumpy, confident, scared. Of course, none of this was apparent. Ramesh rarely revealed emotion, positive or negative. So when the rain didn't stop till mid-day, he calmly cancelled shooting and busied himself with planning for the next day. They worked out shots, planned an alternative route and ways to move machines despite the weather. Only a little voice within him wondered, 'Shit, is this a bad omen?'

An army had moved to Bangalore: director, cinematographer, stars with their spot boys, make-up men and hair-stylists, generators with attendants, cameras with attendants, horses with scythes, construction crew, dress men, cooks, assistants, junior artistes, fighters and dancers. The top crew stayed at the newly opened Ashoka Hotel. All the suites in the hotel—each floor had a corner one—were occupied by the unit. Each star had a suite and a car to himself or herself. This was quite starrily luxurious, especially for Amitabh, who in his last outdoor shoot, *Bombay to Goa*, had been put up at a ramshackle two-star hotel. Amjad and Sanjeev preferred the less spiffy but more functional Hotel Bangalore International. They stayed at HBI with the senior staff. The junior staff—light and production boys—stayed in a third hotel, enroute to the location.

Every morning, a cavalcade of cars left the hotels. The row of Ambassadors resembled a presidential motorcade. There were buses and trucks for crew and equipment. The location was an hour's drive away. The first to depart were usually Ramesh and Divecha at six in the morning. About a hundred and fifty people commuted to Ramanagaram every day. But the size of the operation did not equal confusion. The Sippy production was organized like a Hollywood shoot.

Every evening, the crew got a call sheet with details of the next day, including reporting time, location, shot, costume, and the car number and the time when it would arrive at the hotel for a pick-up. Ramesh and Divecha drove together. While the Ashoka crowd invariably piled into Dharmendra's car, Sanjeev came to the location with his old IPTA pal, Satyen Kappu, and Amjad with his screen shadow, Macmohan. Since Sanjeev was a notoriously late riser, his shots were always scheduled for late morning or afternoon. The drivers had strict instructions that they were not to stop once they had picked up their designated person. There was little room for mess-ups.

October 3rd was the first day of work. *Sholay*'s first shot was a contrite Amitabh returning the keys to the safe to Jaya. This little scene is one of the two in the entire film when Jai speaks to the widow, Radha, and it is the start of their love story. Jaya was three months pregnant at the time. Amitabh had driven her up the bumpy unpaved

'Sholay's first scene was a contrite Amitabh returning the keys to the safe to Jaya.'

road to the Thakur's house in a four-wheeler himself. He wanted to make sure that she was comfortable. He wasn't very enthusiastic about the location, and Jaya's condition was not the only reason why. Amitabh did not think that an untested and unconventional location like Ramanagaram was appropriate for a film like *Sholay*. 'You normally associate dacoits and hired killers with a setting like Rajasthan,' he says, 'and this was totally contrary—green, with big boulders . . . I thought, Ramesh Sippy has really lost it.'

While Jaya struggled with morning sickness and rough roads, Hema struggled with reams of dialogue. Basanti talked non-stop. And Hema just couldn't get the lines and the style right. '*Yeh itna lamba lamba dialogue kaun bolega?* (Who's going to speak such long dialogues?)' she said. 'Surely, you will cut some of it out?' Finally, Javed, who had come for the shoot, enacted the part for her at the hotel, and Basanti tangewali clicked into place for Hema. In the first schedule, Ramesh concentrated on the small scenes: Basanti riding her tanga, Basanti talking to *mausi*, the safe-robbing scene in which Radha catches the two thieves. Slowly Hema and the rest of the unit settled in and got into the stride.

Shooting usually started at seven in the morning and continued until sundown. The set was like a picnic. 'It was great fun,' says Jaya. 'We were like, "Who wants to go back to the hotel? Why can't we just sleep here?"' Even artistes who weren't scheduled to be shooting on a particular day would come to the location to be part of the process. Some of the village was still under construction, and often there were long gaps between shots. The actors whiled away their time playing rummy for one paisa per point. When they got tired, they rested in their air-conditioned make-up rooms, having feasted on the most delicious food.

Bahadur, the cook, imported from Mumbai, rustled up delicacies in his well-stocked kitchen. It was a lavish spread. Every day a banquet—chicken, pigeon, mutton, vegetables—was laid out under a *shamiana* for more than 200 people. The logistics were mind-boggling: a kilo of cooking oil was used; one man ground wheat for chappatis, while two local women cleaned the rice; five cooks with two assistants were at the stove all day long. It was an equal-opportunity feast. Hema carried along South Indian food from the hotel, but the rest of the unit ate what was cooked on location. Long wooden planks were laid out as tables. From stars to spot boys, everybody ate the same food together. Gradually, the locals started joining in too.

The camaraderie on the sets continued after hours as well. After a hard day's work, Ramesh and Divecha would head straight to the Ashoka bar, where Ramesh had one small whiskey with ice and water, and Divecha put away a large one. Then Ramesh eased off the day's tensions with a half-hour massage, followed first by a tub of piping hot water, then a cold shower. He then lined his stomach with a small snack—consommé soup and melba toast—and was ready for the night.

There were parties galore. Suresh Malhotra, the Bangalore distributor, invariably had some local invitation in place. Suresh, a portly man with a thick voice, had a grand passion for both films and food. An old Sippy confidant, he had been distributing their films since *Andaaz*. Master of ceremonies and culinary guide, Suresh organized the evening outings. The *Sholay* unit was making waves, and Bangalore's society ladies were clamouring to have them over. If there wasn't a party, the crew trooped to restaurants—a favourite was a roadside dhaba called Roomali, which served a biryani tasty enough to warm your stomach and your soul. Jaya, slowly swelling, often got late-night cravings for the biryani and Amitabh and Dharmendra were her escorts. On one such midnight meal excursion, their car broke down. They made it back to the hotel in an autorickshaw.

Those staying at Hotel Bangalore International would simply get together in a room and knock back the booze. Hari bhai—nobody called him Sanjeev—was the quintessential night bird. Inordinately fond of drink and food, he would start late and keep going till long after the others had called it a night. His dinner would be repeatedly reheated till he finally ate at two or three in the morning. But Hari bhai never grew mean with alcohol. Instead, his smile grew wider as the night wore on. At some point, he would stop talking altogether and just smile.

The Ashoka gang gathered in the hotel's Kheda bar or in Ramesh's suite. But Javed's routine was a little different. The writer discovered Mehndi Hassan in Bangalore. Amitabh had carried his favourite music with him on location, and introduced Javed to the delights of Hassan's honeyed voice. Whenever Javed was in Bangalore, he would head for Amitabh's room after pack-up to listen to 'Ranjish hi sahi'. Only Hema, aloof and in love, preferred to stay put in her room. Besides, the tanga-riding lessons she had to take after shooting tired her out.

Since Ashoka was a government hotel, the kitchen was closed at 11 p.m. Often everybody just trooped over to HBI and gathered in the lobby restaurant for food and a bit of fun. Sachin, a child star now struggling with awkward adolescence, had been signed on for the role of Ahmed, the blind Imam's son. He would sing at these gatherings. Or Amjad would do some comedy. There would be a bit of dancing too, or some impromptu performances. By midnight, only the *Sholay* unit would be left in the restaurant. Since Anwar—the operative cameraman—didn't drink, it was his job to see that anyone who'd had a bit too much made it to his room safely.

The fun didn't hamper work. It only strengthened relationships. No one had guessed at the magnitude of the success they were heading for, but there was a discernible charge in the unit. Each day brought excitement and the satisfaction of doing top-class work under difficult conditions. For Ramesh and Divecha, there was no break from the labour. Every evening, the two dissected each upcoming frame. Years ago Divecha had taught Ramesh the necessity of planning: During the shooting for *Andaaz,* Divecha had once substituted for the regular cameraman, K. Vaikunth. He arrived on the sets and demanded, 'What's the scene?' Ramesh was surprised. He wasn't used to narrating scenes to cinematographers. But Divecha was a veteran, so he complied. Divecha kept interrupting Ramesh's narration with questions. The process took over half an hour, and Ramesh was annoyed at what he thought was plain interference. But each question cleared confusion and brought some aspect of the scene into clear focus. 'When I went over the scene again,' Ramesh says, 'I could see it in terms of each frame. I saw how important it was to always do my homework. It opened up a whole new way of working.'

Ramesh and Divecha connected wonderfully. Mutual respect bridged the yawning age difference between the two men: Divecha was fifty-five to Ramesh's twenty-nine. Ramesh called him 'Dev saab' and Divecha answered with 'Rameshji.' On the sets, the director and cinematographer were in total harmony. Divecha gave perfect embodiment to the frames in Ramesh's mind. And to get the results he wanted, the way he wanted them, he spared no one. Not even the stars. He wouldn't let the heroes use make-up, and insisted that the stars stand in place for lighting. He had pet names for everyone: Dharmendra was Dhamu and Amitabh, Ami. For Sanjeev he had a more dignified name, Dhuvendra, instead of a two-syllable pet name, because, '*Sach bole to saala great actor hai.* (Truly speaking the fellow's a great actor.)' But when a shot was ready, Divecha didn't shout for the stars by name. He simply blew a horn. The sound summoned the actors.

'Ramesh and Divecha connected wonderfully.'

Divecha's strict demeanour did not last past sunset. He drank only Scotch, which he insisted on buying himself, and joined in the fun, outlasting even the hardiest of partiers, knocking drinks back till three in the morning. Ye⁺ at precisely 6 a.m he would be in the lobby, stone sob.r, ready for a hard day's work. One night, Vinod Khanna, part of another film unit that was also staying at the Ashoka, joined the *Sholay* team at the bar. Vinod got into a discussion with Divecha about lens parts. 'The piece in front of the lens is called an adapter,' Vinod said, 'and the piece behind, a diopter.' 'Not so,' insisted Divecha, quite categorical and reasonable despite all the Scotch he had consumed. 'It's the opposite. The part in front is a diopter and the part behind, an adapter. *Tu cameraman nahin hain, tereko nahin maloom.* (You're not a cameraman, you know nothing about these things.)' The discussion continued well past midnight. A bet of Rs 5000 was made. Finally Divecha forced the hotel staff to open the bookstore. He checked a dictionary. Of course he was right. Since Vinod didn't have Rs 5000 on him, he turned over his Patek Phillipe watch. He left Bangalore the next morning, a wiser man. Anwar, Divecha's operative cameraman, wore the watch for the next eight days but on Divecha's instructions gave it back to Vinod when the unit returned to Mumbai.

Divecha's good sense was responsible for one of the highlights of the film—Jagdeep's Soorma Bhopali. Jagdeep had slipped into the role with ease. Javed had

*'Jagdeep almost
didn't play
Soorma Bhopali.'*

given him a tape of how the dialogue was to be spoken,
and he had perfected the peculiar accent down to Javed's
lisp. But he almost didn't play Soorma Bhopali. One day,
he was hastily summoned to Banglore for shooting, and
then made to cool his heels; Ramesh was busy wrapping
up shots with other artistes. Bored and restless in the
hotel, Jagdeep asked a production manager for Rs 1000
so he could play at the races. The manager refused. A hurt
Jagdeep decided to pack his bags and return to Mumbai;
if this was the way he was going to be treated, the Sippys
could keep the role. Divecha happened to overhear the
exchange. He immediately instructed the manager to give
Jagdeep the money and even offered the actor some of his
own. Jagdeep swallowed his anger, stayed put and did his
scene in one take. The unit doubled over with laughter

while shooting the scene where Soorma Bhopali boasts about beating up Veeru and Jai, oblivious to the fact that the two thugs are standing right behind him.

*

Each day ended with detailed planning for the next. Every shot had its own requirements: horses, dancers, cranes and special contraptions for the camera. These last were designed by Anwar. There was a workshop on the sets, and sometimes Anwar and Aziz bhai would stay up all night supervising the workers. The workers were mostly men from Ramanagaram and the surrounding areas. Only one man among them, a Muslim, understood Hindi. But between Kanada, Hindi and a smattering of English, work got done.

Yet, despite all the planning, things started to go wrong. The first schedule was ten days long, but very little work got done. Some days they managed to get ten shots right, and on others, none at all. In the November schedule, Ramesh completed only one scene. The No Compromise resolve was set in stone. Ramesh and Divecha were like painters trying to perfect their canvas, with G. P. Sippy, a patron of the arts, bankrolling their dreams. Budget and timetables took a backseat.

Sholay's centerpiece—the massacre sequence in which Gabbar obliterates the Thakur's family—was shot in twenty-three days over three schedules. It was a

73

The Thakur's family before the massacre.

complicated scene with several parts: establishing the family, Gabbar's arrival, the shootings, and then the Thakur's arrival on the scene after Gabbar and his men have slaughtered his family and retreated. Half the scene had been shot when the weather changed and the bright sun was replaced by an overcast sky. For two days, the unit waited for the sun to reappear. Then Ramesh realized that the dark clouds were a celestial signal: the overcast look was perfect for the scene. It underlined the tragedy and heightened the sense of doom. It also logically led to the point where the wind starts to build up and dry leaves are blown over the dead bodies. He conferred with Divecha. 'It won't just look good,' Divecha said, 'it will look very good. But what will we do if the sun comes out tomorrow?' Ramesh was willing to take the chance. 'Let's shoot,' he said.

They shot furiously for the next two days. And then the sun popped out again. After a week of work, they had two versions of the same half scene, one against a bright sky and the other against an overcast one. But Ramesh was determined. It was going to be clouds or nothing. So they waited for the gods to do the lighting. With the sun playing hide and seek, there were days when they managed to get only one shot and some when they simply stared at the skies. Filming came to a complete halt.

To speed up the process, Divecha asked Anwar to make a screen to bounce the light off. The screen had to be bigger than the house. Anwar ended up buying all the white cloth in the vicinity to create a seventy-foot-by-hundred-foot screen. He stitched it himself with strong canvas thread. With the huge screen in place, shooting was resumed, but there were shots for which the effect created by the screen wasn't good enough. The gods had to intervene and bring back the clouds.

But it wasn't just the clouds. Nothing seemed to go right. As they neared the end of the sequence, the little boy

Gabbar before he retreats with his men from the Thakur's house.

75

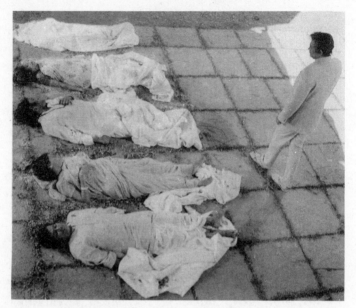

*'Sholay's centrepiece—the massacre sequence—
was shot in twenty-three days.'*

playing the Thakur's grandson, Master Alankar, had
exams. He would lose an academic year if he didn't sit for
them. Ramesh let him go. Then the propeller, which
worked up an appropriate wind to blow the dry leaves
onto the dead bodies, decided to do its own thing. It
wouldn't start when they needed it to. And once it
started, it would just keep going. Finally, an aeronautics
unit near Bangalore built another propeller. It worked
perfectly. The wind blew yellow-brown leaves onto the
bodies and the white shrouds off them, and the Thakur
mounted his horse in a raging fury, ready to look for
Gabbar.

Almost as time-consuming were the sequences of Radha extinguishing the lamps while Jai played his harmonica and watched. These sequences establish the gradual, wordless bonding between the widow and the thief—the sympathy and admiration slowly turning into love. Capturing the right mood was critical. These were two sequences, only about a minute each in the final film, and it took twenty days to shoot them. Ramesh and Divecha decided to do the scenes in 'magic hour', a cinema term for the time between sunset and night. The light that falls during magic hour is dreamlike in its warm golden hue. The director and cinematographer wanted specifically the velvety dusk which arrives at the tail end of the golden hue. A shadowy darkness precedes nightfall, but it is still light enough to show the surrounding silhouettes. Essentially, they had only a few minutes to capture the shot.

The preparations for the shot would begin after lunch. The lights and the camera set-up would be in place well before time. At around five in the evening they would rehearse the shot and the camera movements. Then between six and six-thirty, as the sun started to set, there was total pandemonium. Everyone ran around shouting, trying to get the shot before darkness. Sometimes they would get one shot, sometimes two and very rarely, with great difficulty, a third re-take. But there was never any time to change the set-up.

Ramesh wouldn't settle for anything less than

'The Lady-of-the-Lamps shot became a bit of a joke.'

perfection. Invariably there was always some mess-up. The sun set earlier than they'd expected, a lightman made a mistake, the trolley movement wasn't right, some object was lying where it shouldn't have been. There were times when Jaya lost her cool: 'Ramesh, no one can see me,' she would say. 'It's a long shot, no viewer on the planet is going to be able to see mistakes in continuity.' The answer always was: 'No, no, one more take.' Ramesh dressed each frame. The Lady-of-the-lamps shot became a kind of a joke. It took several schedules to get it right.

In fact, in terms of time taken, each sequence seemed to compete with the next. Ahmed, the blind Imam's son (played by Sachin), for instance, took seventeen days to die. It was a long and complicated sequence, and originally it also included the actual act of killing: meat is roasting in the foreground; Gabbar points a red-hot skewer at the boy and with a gleeful look tells his gang, '*Isko to bahut tadpa tadpa ke maroonga. (I'm going to torture him to death.)*' But this never made it to the final cut. Instead, the scene cuts from Gabbar killing an ant to Ahmed's horse carrying his dead body into the village. The body is a message for the villagers—give up Jai and Veeru. The villagers want the two to leave but Imam saab, wiping away his tears, says he wants them to stay. '*Jaante ho duniya ka sabse bada bojh kya hota hai?*' he says. '*Baap ke kandhe par bete ka janaza . . . Aaj*

Jai plays his harmonica and watches Radha extinguishing the lamps.

79

*'Gabbar points a red-hot skewer at the boy . . . This scene never
made it to the final cut.'*

poochhoonga apne khuda se ki mujhe aur bete kyun
nahin diye shaheed hone ke liye. (You know what is the
greatest burden to bear? . . . The weight of a son's corpse
on a father's shoulder . . . I will ask God today why he did
not give me more sons to be martyred.)' The scene is a
remarkable mix of drama and patriotism, Hangal
bringing to it the right mix of helpless grief and touching
pride.

For the shot of the horse bringing in Ahmed's body,
Ramesh had decided to use a duplicate for Sachin, but the
actor insisted that he could do it himself. During the
scene, Veeru and Jai pick up the body and lay it on the
ground. Just before the shot began, Amitabh whispered
to the young Sachin that he should keep his body stiff. A

loose, limp body would be hard to carry. Sachin nodded in agreement. Once the shot was canned, surprised by Sachin's exactly-right rigidity and his obvious professionalism, Amitabh asked him, 'How many films have you done?'

'About sixty,' Sachin replied nonchalantly.

Amitabh's jaw fell. 'Since when have you been working?'

Sachin said, 'Nineteen sixty-two.'

After that Amitabh treated Sachin like a senior.

Hangal, who had done extensive work with IPTA, was also a veteran actor, but he was a newcomer to films—before *Sholay*, he had done only a few, select films like *Guddi* and *Namak Haram*, preferring instead the rigours of theatre. But he had already earned a formidable reputation and prominent directors turned to him when they had an important character role in their films. For the sequence of Ahmed's death, Hangal had flown in from Nepal, where he was shooting near Mount Everest for Dev Anand's *Ishq Ishq Ishq*. The dates were back to back, and Dev Anand had arranged for a helicopter to bring Hangal from his location to Kathmandu so that he could make it to Bangalore in time.

Hangal had prepared extensively for his role as a blind man, using what he calls 'psycho-technique'. He imagined the feeling of blindness by going back millions of years to the beginnings of evolution, when all life that was to come was contained in sightless single-celled

'Hangal prepared extensively for his role as a blind man.'

organisms swimming in the dark waters. Once there, he would grope and search for sight. He kept the searching movement through the scene of Ahmed's death.

Tarachand Barjatya was on location when they shot the scene and was greatly impressed by what he saw. So much so that he wrote Hangal a letter saying that he had never seen another scene like it. But Hangal wasn't satisfied with his performance. That night, at dinner, he told Ramesh that he felt something was missing. 'How can it be?' Ramesh asked, 'I okayed the take.' 'No, it's not complete,' Hangal insisted. 'Well,' Ramesh said, 'if you aren't satisfied, we'll reshoot.' Later Ramesh took Hangal to see the rushes—on most evenings, after pack-up, Ramesh would see the rushes at a local theatre. After they'd seen the rushes, he asked Hangal: '*Bolo Hangal saab, kaisa laga?* (Tell me, Hangal saab, what do you think?)' Hangal had to agree that it was okay.

*

Co-ordinating horses, actors and cameras was difficult enough. Then local extortionists showed up. Ramesh was shooting a sequence in the village square when a production assistant announced that four students had arrived and wanted to speak with him. Ramesh told him to make them wait till the shooting was finished, and he carried on working. By the evening he had forgotten all about them. Then the assistant reminded him that they were still waiting. When Ramesh sat down with them, he could see belligerence on their faces. Clearly, this wasn't a social visit.

Their demands were simple: 'Stop shooting or we'll burn the set down.' A Karnataka-Maharashtra language dispute was going on, and they wanted the Mumbai filmmaker to go away. Ramesh was taken aback. He tried reasoning with them. After all, *Sholay* was providing livelihood to hundreds of locals. But the boys were adamant. Shooting had to stop. The next day, it became apparent why. They wanted Rs 50,000. It was plain and simple extortion.

Ramesh refused. 'Burn the set,' he told them. 'I'm not stopping work.' By night their demands had come down to Rs 20,000. Ramesh still played hard ball. By day three, they were willing to settle for Rs 10,000. By then, it was obvious that these were amateurs with 'little *dum*'. Ramesh talked to the commissioner of police, who organized a sting operation. The students were given marked notes, immediately nabbed and thrown into jail. Two days later, farmers from the neighbouring village showed up. They were the boys' fathers. They cried and begged Ramesh to forgive their sons; the boys were immature and foolish but not criminal, they pleaded. Ramesh dropped the case. Eventually the blackmailers ended up as unit hands.

But even the extortionists were easier to deal with than a miffed wife. One night, after a hard day's work, Ramesh was woken up by the ringing of the telephone. It was Geeta calling from Mumbai. Geeta often accompanied Ramesh on his schedules and was very much part of the unit, joining the crew on location on most days. This was one of the rare times she had stayed away. She did not ask about work as she normally did. She sounded angry. There was only one question: 'Have you read the latest *Stardust*?' Ramesh hadn't. 'Read it and call me back,' she said and put the phone down.

Ramesh rarely had time for film magazines. But this sounded serious. So he called for the magazine, flipped through it and called Mumbai.

'I've gone through the magazine. What are you talking about?'

'Naturally. Why would *you* find it?"

'Where would I find what?'

'Page forty.'

And Geeta hung up again. Ramesh turned to page forty and almost keeled over with laughter. There was a detailed article about his alleged affair with Parveen Babi. He had never met the young, upcoming actress. Husband and wife disagreed on how to deal with the article. Ramesh wanted to ignore it. Geeta insisted that he issue a denial. Finally the Bachchans spoke to the editor of the magazine, Ingrid Alburquque, who was a close friend. *Stardust* printed a clarification, but six months later.

*

Gabbar Singh was not having a good day. It was Amjad's first day of shooting. They were starting with the scene in which he is introduced. His first line was, '*Kitne aadmi the?*' All his life had led to this moment. The years of theatre rehearsals, knocking on doors for acting jobs, sweating it out as an assistant—the Gabbar role had made all that seem worthwhile. Amjad was a second-generation film actor and an award-winning theatre actor. He had struggled for ten years and honed his craft to perfection. His army fatigues, picked up from Mumbai's Chor Bazaar, had the right weathered look. His teeth were blackened. His face was appropriately grimy. He had lived the part for the last few months. But now, when it was time to deliver, he just could not get it right.

Gabbar had to mince *tambaku* as he talked. The

motion of one hand grinding against another added to his menace. It was supposed to be his habit. But Amjad could not make it look casual. He would grind the tobacco, speak a few lines, look around awkwardly and then return to grinding. He was nervous and it showed; his hands were stiff, his movements seemed rehearsed, and his dialogue delivery was shaky. There was nothing natural about his performance; Gabbar was a stranger to Amjad.

Ramesh kept talking to him, trying to help him get his lines right. They struggled for two days. After forty-odd takes, both Ramesh and Divecha decided that the actor needed a break. Divecha told Amjad to keep his costume on and just sit on the sets. '*Tu apne aap ko season kar de.* (Season yourself.)' Amjad cried that night. His father was in hospital fighting cancer. His son was only a month old. His family's hopes were pinned on this film.

For the rest of the schedule, Amjad lived in the fatigues, trying to become Gabbar. He wrote often to his wife but never shared with her the extent of his trauma. All he wrote was: 'I'm very impatient . . . I don't know . . . I hope I can do it.' Since he didn't drink, he would spend the evenings nursing endless cups of tea. Through the entire schedule, he didn't do a single shot.

In the next schedule, Amjad was more prepared. He got it right in the first few takes. He was living his character, and would stay in costume even when he was not shooting. But some members of the unit, unable to

'Gabbar Singh was not having a good day . . . Gabbar was a stranger to Amjad.'

forget his earlier awkwardness, didn't seem to think this was enough. Besides, Amjad was the only new face in a sea of superstars—even Bachchan, originally the underdog, was now red hot—and slowly talk started in the unit that perhaps Ramesh had made a mistake. Amjad was miscast. He would turn out to be a liability. The murmurs grew, till it became impossible even for Salim and Javed, who had been the most keen to have Amjad as Gabbar, to ignore them. Anxious, perhaps, to not be seen as people responsible for ruining the film, they spoke to Ramesh about it. 'If you aren't satisfied with Amjad, change him,' they said. For a few days the unit was rocked by rumours that Amjad was getting the boot. But Ramesh finally put his foot down. Only Amjad

87

would play Gabbar.

Amjad found out about the rumours much later. But the incident sowed the seeds of misunderstanding between him and Salim-Javed. He could not understand why two people who had ardently recommended him for the role had then tried to get him thrown out. He saw it as a move to sabotage his career. The hurt stayed with him till his death. Salim-Javed gave birth to the Amjad myth but they never worked with him again.

*

The *Sholay* unit had a ten- to fifteen-day schedule in Bangalore every month, from October 1975 to May 1976. Each time they managed to get some work done,

'Salim-Javed gave birth to the Amjad myth but they never worked with him again.'

The main star cast of *Sholay*, except Jaya Bhaduri, with Ramesh Sippy.

An army of cast and crew in Ramanagaram

The four male lead actors : Amitabh, Dharmendra, Sanjeev and Amjad

Thakur Baldev Singh (above) with the residents of Ramgarh, and Gabbar Singh (right) at the roasting pit in his den: to Ramesh Sippy, *Sholay* was their film

Veeru at the temple
cheating Basanti as
'God'

Basanti praying for the man of her dreams as her husband

Jai, defending
Ramgarh against
Gabbar's men

Radha on her way to the temple

Shooting the *'Angrezon ke zamaane ke jailer'* sequence

Jai, Veeru and the jailer's *'jaasoos'*

Veeru and Jai, cheerful in jail

Asrani in full flow as the jailer

Veeru and Jai decide to settle down in Ramgarh

Gabbar's den — shooting the *'Kitne aadmi the'* scene

but not enough. The delays were further compounded because 70mm required that each shot be taken twice. After seven months of work, hardly one-third of the film had been shot. *Sholay* had been planned as a six-month project. Nobody imagined that eventually it would take so long that Macmohan, playing Sambha, one of the smallest roles in the film, would travel twenty-seven times from Mumbai to Bangalore.

Ramesh retained his famous cool. He had a grand vision of *Sholay* and he wasn't going to let delays force him to make compromises. As the budget soared beyond the original one crore, G. P. Sippy did make the occasional noise. 'What the hell is going on?' he would ask. But he never pulled the plug. He was a gambler going for the big one. The funds kept flowing.

In May 1974, the crew assembled once again in Ramanagaram. Jaya had delivered in March. Her plump, glowing-with-motherhood face hardly suited the character of the emaciated widow Ramesh had in mind. Obviously it wasn't going to work. Ramesh then made a significant decision. He gathered his crew and said, 'Look, there's a lot going wrong here. I'm going to cancel this schedule, primarily for Jaya. But all of you call your secretaries and shift your dates around. Because the next time I come to Bangalore, I want to finish the film. It may take one month or two or three for us to get everyone together, but the next time we come, we go back with the film.'

Everybody agreed. The schedule was cancelled. Instead the cast took off to London for a holiday. Ramesh's brother, Ajit, played host. Shooting for *Sholay* did not resume until September 1974.

CHAPTER 6

BAHUT YAARANA LAGTA HAI

The sniggering had started. Tall tales floated back to Mumbai from Bangalore about the endless delays, the mounting expenses, the foolhardy perfectionist attitude. The film industry was quick to pick up these stories and exaggerate them. *Sholay* had dwarfed the industry with its scale, prestige and ambition. It would be fun to watch it fall. Failure is as important and welcome in Bollywood as success, depending on which side you are on; in an industry where ninety per cent of the films flop, the dictum is: 'It is not enough that I succeed. You must fail.' And lately, the box office gods had been favouring the Sippys too much.

The rumours spread like a rot: a start-to-finish project wasn't aloft after seven months; money was being sucked into *Sholay* like matter into a black hole; the Sippys were regretting having spent so much money putting up a village in Bangalore, because Mumbai's Chandivili

Studio or China Creek would have done just as well. Back in Mumbai, Ramesh bumped into the actor Jeetendra. 'You guys are still shooting *Sholay?*' Jeetendra asked incredulously. 'I've finished three films!'

Ramesh remained unruffled. He had never been an assembly-line filmmaker. For him, cinema was not about speed or success or stardom. Ramesh had what Salim calls 'the clarity of authority'. The film was etched in his mind. If it took two years to make it a reality, so be it. He concentrated his energies on planning for the months ahead. It was going to be an arduous few months, and organization was essential if they were to finish the film.

Meanwhile, more music was created and recorded. On a visit to London, Ramesh and Geeta heard a Demi Russo number at Ajit's. It had an infectious beat that could cross over to Hindi film audiences. Geeta suggested creating a song inspired by the number and weaving it into the film. Ramesh agreed. Back in India, he played the song for Pancham and Bakshi, who didn't take long to adapt the tune for their purpose, and *'Mehbooba'* was created. Since no other singer could match the raunchy beat, Pancham decided to sing it himself. But what would be an appropriate situation for the song? There was little scope in a no-nonsense, earthy action film like *Sholay* for a foot-tapping number with an obviously Western beat.

The team fell back on a tried and tested Hindi-film formula. Gabbar would follow a weapon-buying spree with a decadent night under the stars. Gypsies would do

'Ramesh had what Salim calls "the clarity of authority".'

'Mehbooba'. It was also the perfect way to squeeze in a sexy Helen number. Javed hated it. It was a completely generic situation, the villain watching a semi-clad dancer. It was too filmi, and out of character for Gabbar. This was perhaps the only time that he and Ramesh had heated discussions. But when Javed heard the song, he did a volte-face. *'Aap kyon ise kisi aur se gawa rahen hain?* (Why are you getting someone else to sing it in the film?)' he asked Ramesh. 'It's a hit song. Can't we create a situation between Dharmendra and Hema Malini?' Ramesh and the others didn't think the song would work for Veeru and Basanti. The gypsy idea was the best. So *'Mehbooba'* stayed and, of course, became a hit.

While the songs were being finalized, Asrani's *'Angrezon ke zamane ka jailer'* sequence was shot at Rajkamal studios in Mumbai. Asrani had the jailer's fumbling walk and talk down pat. He had everyone present at the shoot, including G. P. Sippy and Salim-Javed, in splits and his first take was okayed. With Asrani in such brilliant form, the sequence, it seemed, could even be canned ahead of schedule. But the following day shooting was cancelled. The jailer was to have six policemen walking behind him. On day two, only four of the junior artistes turned up. The other two were busy with another shoot. Amitabh, Dharmendra and over fifty junior artistes were ready to shoot. But Ramesh inisisted: 'No, I want those two.' By 12.30, it became clear that it would not be possible to extricate them from the other shoot. Ramesh announced pack-up. Junior artistes were as critical as the stars. Eventually the sequence was shot over five days.

The secretaries of all the stars were busy too, shuffling

'Mehbooba': 'The perfect way to squeeze in
a sexy Helen number.'

dates. The original dates allotted to *Sholay* had been used up and new ones were needed, that too at a stretch. This 'adjustment' with other producers—so vital in Bollywood—required manipulation at a Machiavellian level, but everyone did finally 'adjust'. The Sippys were, after all, kings of the heap, and for almost all the stars involved, *Sholay* was priority number one. By end-September, the *Sholay* unit was back where it belonged: in Ramanagaram.

*

The songs were as hard to execute as the scenes. They took several days over many schedules and involved hundreds of dancers, special camera devices, a tanga and even a train. As usual, Ramesh pulled out all stops.

'*Yeh dosti*' was a twenty-one-day endeavor. The song establishes the friendship between Veeru and Jai. Its easy camaraderie is the foundation of the film. The cheer of the happy version perfectly offsets the dirge-like version at Jai's death. It was decided that a motorcycle with a sidecar would capture the spirit of the male-bonding anthem. But to shoot the entire song from a moving vehicle was static and limiting. So they built a special contraption, which would enable the crew to use different kinds of camera movements.

The contraption allowed for varied camera angles. Divecha could start on a tight close-up of one character,

'Asrani had the jailer's fumbling walk and talk down pat.'

pull back, move around to include both and then turn almost 180 degrees to the other side. Shots like these would make the audience feel that they were traveling with Veeru and Jai. But they weren't easy to get. First the bike would be fitted onto the contraption, and then the whole paraphernalia would move along with the camera and tracks and a low trolley moving up and down. Coordinating the elements—reflectors, sun-guns, speakers—needed minute organization and the patience of a priest. There were frequent mechanical faults: the towing hook would come off, or the pulling vehicle would get so heated up that it wouldn't start.

None of which stopped Ramesh and choreographer

P.L. Raj from planning even more intricate moves. '*Yeh dosti*', they decided, would end with the sidecar breaking away, doing a short solo run and then coming together with the motorcycle again. It was a neat gimmick. If only they could make it work. The sidecar had to be pulled away from the motorcycle without making the pulling obvious. And then there was the toughest part: the two had to reunite after separating on a fork on the road. They attached the sidecar to the camera on a trolley and rehearsed the shot with Amitabh, who was riding the motorcycle. It all depended on his sense of timing, because he was on a moving vehicle while the camera was on a fixed trolley. Amitabh would have to time it to perfection—start at the right moment, and accelerate or slow down according to the movement of the camera. Amazingly, he brought in the motorcycle for a smooth, perfect docking on the very first take. It was a miracle. The unit broke into a spontaneous applause and even the normally reticent Ramesh jumped off the camera stand and hugged Amitabh.

'*Koi haseena*' needed a different kind of co-ordination. It has a miffed Basanti speeding along on her tanga, and an apologetic Veeru on a bicycle trying to woo her back. In the background is a train chugging on cheerily, sending out lazy spumes of smoke into the sky. The lyrics made the train essential:

Koi haseena jab rooth jaati hai to aur bhi haseen ho

97

'Yeh dosti': 'A motorcycle with a sidecar would capture the spirit
of the male-bonding anthem.'

jati hai
Station se gadi jab chhoot jaati hai to ek do teen ho
    jati hai
(When a pretty woman gets angry, she becomes even
    prettier
When a train leaves the station, it speeds away, one
    two three...)

The camera had to move along and follow the tanga,

98

the cycle, and the local train, which passed through Ramanagaram once a day at 7.50 a.m. The timing of the train was inflexible. And since Dharmendra and Hema were leaving the same day for another shooting, losing the shot meant that it would be canned only in the next schedule.

The crew was in place by 7 a.m. The shot had been rehearsed several times; the trolleys were in place; Hema, in the tanga, and Dharmendra, on his cycle, were ready. Then it was discovered that a crucial ingredient was missing: the flowers that went into Hema's hair. She had already done part of the song with flowers embellishing her hairdo. The shot couldn't be done without them.

A neat gimmick: the sidecar breaking away for a solo run.

'Where are the flowers?' Ramesh asked. At that precise moment, they were heading toward Bangalore on a truck that had gone to collect breakfast for the crew. Obviously somebody had miscalculated. Panic ensued. It was perhaps one of the few times that Ramesh screamed. Precious minutes were ticking by and there was little they could do. Khalish Lukhnavi, a mild-mannered, God-fearing assistant from G. P. Sippy's directing days, was in charge of continuity. He went white and prayed hard. 'I thought I would have a heart attack,' he recalls.

Seven minutes before the train passed by, the truck returned with both breakfast and flowers. The flowers were rushed from the truck to the tanga, where Hema waited. They were hurriedly fixed in her hair, the vehicle carrying the camera was rolled back, the tanga moved and at exactly the right moment, the train passed by. The relief was palpable. Yet another crisis had been averted.

The Holi song was an epic exercise with dozens of dancers, junior artistes, colours, and a mela atmosphere, complete with a Ferris wheel and a merry-go-round. It took about twenty days to get the entire song right.

'Jab tak hai Jaan', the catchy pre-climax number, was shot on the rocks in Gabbar's den. Basanti is dancing to save Veeru's life. Sambha has a gun cocked at Veeru and Gabbar's orders to Basanti are: 'Jab tak tere paon chalenge, uski saans chalegi; jab tere paon ruke to yeh bandook chalegi. (As long as your feet move, he breathes; when your feet stop moving, the gun breathes.)' Hema

A miffed Basanti, and Veeru trying to woo her back.

was a consummate dancer, trained in classical dance for years. For her, the steps were easy. But the setting was difficult. Basanti's struggle to keep dancing under the scorching sun had to look real to be effective. Ramesh wanted to shoot the song in summer but Hema protested. 'Why not in January?' she asked. 'Because,' replied Ramesh, 'I want that expression on your face of torture due to the extreme heat.'

Ramesh prevailed. The song was shot in May. But Bangalore's weather played hooky. The days were steaming hot and the nights brought rain. The water would make the rocks slushy. It looked damp instead of dry and broiling. So every morning, the production unit

101

would hasten the drying process with fans and blowers. By mid-morning the shooting would start. The rocks would be scorching hot. Hema was uncomfortable dancing with pads on her feet and did most of her shots without them. But for the long shots, Ramesh insisted on the pads. 'I don't want you to torture yourself unnecessarily,' he said. Hema's spot boy used to hover at the edge of the frame, ready to splash water on her feet as soon as the shot was done.

There was more agony. Halfway through the song, Sambha throws a bottle on the rocks and Basanti dances on glass. They used plastic as mock glass, but for the actual bottle-breaking shot, it had to be the real thing. Hema's feet, already blistered, caught a few splinters when the bottle shattered. But she, literally, put her best foot forward and delivered.

*

Handling prickly egos and star tempers was as important as camera placements. While shooting the climax, Dharmendra came to Ramesh with a suggestion on how to do a particular shot. Ramesh and Divecha had already worked out the details and Ramesh brushed off Dharmendra's suggestion. Paaji flared— 'Kya yaar, meri baat toh tum kabhi sunte hi nahin ho! (What's this, yaar, you never listen to anything I say!)' Ramesh, taken aback, said, 'Fine, let's do the shot both ways.' It was done once according to Ramesh's and Divecha's original plan. Then Ramesh turned to Dharmendra, 'Okay, now let's see. You think the camera should first track right and then zoom in on Gabbar?' Dharmendra looked a little sheepish and said, 'Forget it, yaar, let's keep your shot.'

In the climax sequence, Gabbar holds Basanti's arm and menacingly delivers the lines: '*Dekho chhamiya, zyada nakhre mat karo humse, nahin to ye gori chamdi hai na—saare badan se khurach khurach ke utaar doonga.* (Look, girl, don't put on your airs with me, or this fair skin of yours—I'll scrape it all off you.)' By now, Amajd had settled in. The insecurities of the early schedules were replaced by confidence and he wore

'Jab tak hai jaan': *Ramesh said, 'I want that expression on your face of torture due to the extreme heat.'*

103

Gabbar's persona like a second skin. In the heat of the performance, Amjad gripped Hema's arm a little too tightly. It hurt. But the shot was canned and the crew moved on to the next one. By the evening, Hema's arm was sore and the bruises showed. At the dinner table, Dharmendra could barely control his anger.

Dharmendra, or Paaji, as everyone called him, was in love with Hema Malini. The attraction between them, so obvious in *Seeta aur Geeta*, was blossoming slowly but surely into a full-blown affair. They were both young, beautiful and at the peak of their careers. Love was a foregone conclusion. But as in any love story, there were complications. Dharmendra was married and had children, and Hema's mother, who exerted enormous influence on her life, did not approve of him. Sanjeev Kumar, an eligible bachelor, had already proposed to Hema during *Seeta aur Geeta*. He had been rejected, but hadn't given up hope. Remarkably, little of the underlying drama in the love triangle surfaced during the shooting, though there was always the possibility that some careless word or gesture would unleash something unpleasant. (Thankfully, Jeetendra, another successful hero also rumoured to be interested in Hema, was not part of the *Sholay* cast.)

Hema, professional to the core, gave little trouble. Since she hardly had any scenes with Sanjeev, there were no problems in that quarter. But Dharmendra wore his heart on his sleeve. When he and Hema shot romantic

104

'Gabbar holds Basanti's arm . . . By the evening, Hema's arm was sore and the bruises showed.'

sequences, he paid the light boys to make mistakes so he could embrace her again and again. Dharmendra and the light boys had a perfectly worked-out code language: when he pulled his ear, the light boys would make a mistake—mess up the trolley movement or make a reflector fall—but when he touched his nose, they okayed the shot. The fee was Rs 100 per retake. On a good day, the light boys returned from the day's shooting richer by Rs 2,000.

Dharmendra asked Ramesh to play cupid. 'Please say nice things about me to her,' he told Ramesh, 'I want to marry her.' Ramesh was Hema's confidant. She trusted him. And gradually she too began to admit her feelings for Dharmendra. Soon Paaji was spending more and more evenings in Hema's room. One day after pack-up the crew was hanging out together at HBI, sharing a few drinks, laughs and stories, when Dharam and Hema walked in together. It was obvious to everyone there that they were a couple.

But the insecurities of being a married man in love with the country's most eligible single woman got to the star. His alcohol intake was in direct proportion to his passion, and by the end of the Bangalore schedules, he was tipsy even during the day. He had taken to carrying coconut water with him to the sets. It was, of course, spiked. When Hema wasn't required for shooting, he would make excuses not to come on location. One night, after a long drinking binge, he decided to punish himself by walking to the location. He left the hotel sometime after midnight and kept walking. The next morning there was panic. The crew was ready to leave and Dharmendra had disappeared. They found him in Ramanagaram, sleeping like a baby in one of the make-up rooms. He had walked several kilometers.

Like Hari bhai, Dharmendra rarely turned mean with alcohol. In fact, he became more affectionate and child-like. He caused a few delays and some chaos but was never difficult. Quite the opposite, in fact. The climax shot required him to throw the counterfeit coin—which Jai used to arrive at decisions—in anger and sorrow after Jai's death. Production had made six counterfeit double-headed coins for retakes. But in that rocky terrain, once a coin was thrown it was almost impossible to retrieve it. Dharmendra was a little tipsy, and it became apparent that he might require more than six retakes. Khalish, growing more nervous by the minute, quickly collected as many twenty-five-paise coins as he could find. He asked Dharmendra to be careful. For the long shots Khalish would hand Dharmendra the twenty-five-paise coins, and for the close-ups, the special double-headed ones. Dharmendra was all co-operation, and the shot was canned with one counterfeit coin to spare.

All this passion wasn't Dharmendra's fault, really. As Hema says, 'It was such a beautiful atmosphere that everyone was in love...even the old cameraman.' Pran,

'Dharmendra paid the light boys to make mistakes so he could embrace Hema again and again.'

who was in Bangalore for another shoot, had introduced Divecha to a local girl. She was seventeen. Divecha, in his mid-fifties, fell hopelessly in love. But it wasn't the typical film-industry 'it-doesn't-count-on-location' fling. Despite extreme stress on the home front, Divecha remained committed to the girl till he died in 1978.

*

The *tanki* scene had been discussed but the dialogues weren't written yet. It was the highlight of Dharmendra's role in the film: a smashed Veeru climbs to the top of a water tank and threatens to commit suicide unless Basanti's *mausi* promises to marry them. Salim and Javed were in Bangalore, and as usual, after the scene and the dialogues had been thrashed out, the actual writing was left to Javed. He kept putting it off. The shooting was some time away and there didn't seem to be any tearing hurry. Between shooting and partying, the next few days flew by. It was time for Javed to return to Mumbai and the scene hadn't been written yet. He started writing it on the way to the Bangalore airport. But traffic was easy and they reached the airport before it was finished. So they parked the car outside. Javed sent an assistant to check in for him while he put the paper on the hood of the car and scribbled the lines furiously. Boarding had been announced and Javed was still writing. He made the flight with only minutes to spare. In a few months his hastily written lines would be playing on record players in homes across India.

While the stars and the writers flew in and out of Bangalore, Ramesh and the technical crew virtually lived there, some out of necessity and others out of choice. When Sachin's shooting had been wrapped up, for instance, he asked one of the assistant directors to take a message to Ramesh: he wanted to stay on. Ramesh agreed, thinking that perhaps the boy had relatives or friends in Bangalore. But the reason why Sachin wanted to stay was not that at all. 'I just want to come on the sets and observe. I won't disturb you,' the fifteen-year-old told Ramesh. So Sachin, who had dreamt of direction even when he was a child star, became an assistant. He would sit behind Ramesh and watch him direct. Soon he had picked up enough to help: he would pick up property or help in continuity or in the dress department. But mostly he tagged along with Ramesh's other de facto assistant, Amjad.

Amjad wasn't doing any other films at the time. So like Ramesh, he settled in Bangalore. His wife, Shaila, and son, Shadab, would come to stay with him sometimes. He lived in his army fatigues, but since he wasn't shooting every day he started taking on production work. He had already assisted K. Aasif and was familiar with the rigours of shooting. Soon he was practically running the second unit, armed with a clapboard and continuity sheets.

The tanki scene: 'Javed's hastily written lines would be playing in homes across India.'

The other stars were madly busy. Dates for *Sholay* had required much juggling and there were several other films that had to be accommodated. Some producers who needed to finish projects simply came to Bangalore. Hema and Dharmendra dubbed for producer Premji's *Dost* in Bangalore. Amitabh was dividing time between a Devan Varma production and *Sholay*. Manmohan Desai put up a set for *Dharamveer* in Bangalore. Since *Dharamveer* had Dharmendra playing a prince in a Roman-style thigh-length tunic, the star had to stay in shape. So while he continued boozing late into the night, he also started waking up at 4:30 a.m. to work out. One day, Amitabh happened to catch him pumping iron at dawn. 'Paaji,' he said, shaking his head in amazement, '*how* do you do it?'

But despite the hectic schedules and the fact that what was initially planned as a six-month shooting had stretched to well over a year, there was no sense of fatigue or boredom. The energy of the early days was palpable even a year later. Working and living together had created a familial bonding that perhaps would have been

'The last shot done in the village was Jai's death scene.'

111

'Hari bhai, the consummate actor, had forgotten that the Thakur had no arms.'

impossible had the shooting been done in Mumbai. 'We lived the film,' says Jaya, 'and it wasn't just time spent as in days. It was emotional time. We were all deeply involved.'

In end-January 1974, the *Sholay* unit bid good bye to Ramanagaram. It had become a second home. They had spent so much time there that a light man named Mehboob had married a local girl. The last shot done in the village was Jai's death scene. It was a heart-breaking scene, made more poignant by their imminent departure. Toward the end of the scene, Radha looks at the Thakur—the glimmer of hope in her barren life has been extinguished—and breaks down on his shoulder. While shooting, Hari bhai came to Ramesh and in a soft, anguished tone, said, 'I can see in Radha's eyes that she is devastated . . . she was married to my son . . . and then I was marrying her off (to Jai) and then this tragedy happens . . . I feel so bad for her . . . Can I take her in my arms and comfort her?' Ramesh looked at him and in a deadpan voice replied, 'What arms?' Hari bhai, the consummate actor, turned away, embarrassed. Completely involved in the scene and moved by Radha's grief, he had forgotten that the Thakur had no arms.

With this final scene most of the film was complete. All that remained to be shot were the 'Mehbooba' song and the opening train sequence.

CHAPTER 7

JO DAR GAYA, SAMJHO MAR GAYA

Ramesh wanted epic action. He visualized spectacular violence with a ballet-like beauty and grace. Salim-Javed had gone as far as their imagination would take them. *Sholay* had a gruelling train sequence, lengthy horse chases, and an ambitious attack on the village. Men had to fall off cliffs and horses, collapse in the dust. Even the heroine had to manoeuvre her tanga furiously. Action was the *raison d'etre* of the film. But who could translate the scribbled lines into screen images?

The early seventies were kinder, gentler movie times. Occasionally bullets flew around a bit and some blood was seen on screen, but action was mostly a 'last-reel' affair. That is, after thirteen reels of love songs and emotional intrigue, the baddies would create some mischief. A few punches, coordinated to the sound of *dhishum-dhishum*, would be exchanged, there might be a chase and some guns, but it was all over in a few minutes.

The complicated train sequence: 'Action was the raison d'etre
of the film.'

Action was mostly small and cartoonish and not taken
very seriously.

Ramesh considered the heavyweight action directors
of the time and eventually handed the reins to Azeem bhai
and Mohammed Hussain. Azeem bhai, known only by
his first name, was a veteran. He had worked on classics
like *Ganga Jamuna* and had a fleet of well-trained
stuntmen working for him. It wasn't unusual for Azeem
bhai to have as many as five shootings running
simultaneously. Hussain, on the other hand, had directed
successful stunt movies. Together they were to head a
second unit that would can most of the action shots while
Ramesh's unit concentrated on the talkie portions.

One of the first action sequences to be shot was the title

sequence, in which Ramlal and the police inspector ride from the train station to the Thakur's house. Badri Prasad Verma, who provided the horses and did some duplicate work, and his son Bhikoo, one of Azeem bhai's stuntmen, did the riding. Duplicates like Badri and Bhikoo were extremely important: the regular actors were not used to the kind of rigours required for the action scenes in *Sholay*; most of the films that they had done before hadn't put such a premium on action. Satyen Kappu, for instance, successfully wrestled with emotional scenes but threw up his hands when it came to horses. 'Sorry, Ramesh,' he said, '*mujhe maaf kardo* (you'll have to excuse me).'

Kappu wasn't the only one. Though most of *Sholay's* cast had been given riding lessons in Mumbai—they rode early morning on Juhu beach—handling the horses on location was proving to be trickier than expected. Around twenty horses had been carted by truck from Mumbai to Bangalore. The Mumbai horses, trained for film, were unfazed by the bright lights, the technical equipment and even the blasts. They responded to commands like 'action' and 'cut' like professional actors. But the Bangalore horses, twenty of them, on loan from the Mounted Police and the Mysore Race Club, were amateurs. One was a chestnut-brown mare named Nefertiti after the Egyptian princess. Nefertiti was a racehorse, used to running long distances. Sudden noises, lights, and the sight of large equipment made her nervous

116

and she threw off her riders with alarming regularity. Not surprisingly, the crew named her 'Nafrati', because she hated anyone who sat on her.

No one escaped Nafrati's wrath. While shooting the Thakur-Gabbar chase sequence, she threw off Amjad five times, once even stepping on his back. Once she bucked at a sudden noise and dislodged Dharmendra. And Viju Khote spent most of the shooting surviving Nafrati.

Viju's seven and a half minutes on screen required two weeks of work. First they made him Kaalia: when even the darkest shade of foundation—Negro Black—couldn't get him dark enough, the make-up man mixed Negro Black with *ambar* powder. Then they gave him appropriately menacing daku-style eyebrows: pencilling couldn't sufficiently thicken Viju's almost non-existent eyebrows, so a false moustache was cut in half and pasted above his eyes. And as if the elaborate makeover hadn't exhausted and disoriented him, when he started shooting, Nafrati set about breaking his bones. In the first week itself, she threw him off six times.

The action department made sure that there were several horses of the same colour. There were four white horses and five black ones. But there was only one chestnut-brown fiend—Nafrati. Since Kaalia was riding Nafrati for the first scene of the dakus entering the village, he had no choice but to ride her for the subsequent scenes. But Nafrati wouldn't yield an inch. She played temperamental diva from the first shot to the last.

117

The village shot required Kaalia to carry a rifle. At one point in the sequence, Kaalia reaches for the rifle and Jai shoots him in the arm. The production unit didn't have a saddle holster for the rifle, so they improvised—they got an ordinary rifle case and tied it to the buckle under the flap of the saddle. The case would hang down and they could put the rifle in it. But they hadn't factored in Nafrati. Every time the mare saw a rifle or a stick, she would buck. If the rifle as much as touched her leg, she'd start running wild. There was only one solution: Viju had to position his leg in such a way that the rifle didn't touch the mare. In the film, there are long shots where Kaalia is riding and one leg is protruding out at a strange angle, keeping the rifle away from Nafrati.

It wasn't just rifles that made Nafrati nervous. She didn't like water either. For one shot the dakus had to ride a bridge over a pond. Nafrati refused. When Viju's coaxing didn't work, Azeem bhai stepped in. But as he turned Nafrati away from the water, she accidentally stepped into a thorn bush, bucked and deposited the dhoti-clad Viju into a bed of thorns. He couldn't move at all and lay there helpless and in agony till he was extricated from the bush.

The last shoot of the schedule included a sweeping crane shot. The crane was placed behind the three horsemen. Through the shot, the crane would move up to encompass the dakus and the entire village. When Nafrati glimpsed something large moving behind her, she started

118

bucking up and down in the best rodeo fashion.
Meanwhile, stuntmen shouted instructions at a
bewildered Viju: '*Kheench ke rakkho*, tight, tight.' He
tried, but was thrown off, this time onto a stone. That, he
decided, was the last straw. 'I'm not sitting on that horse
again,' he told Ramesh. No amount of coaxing or
pleading would change Viju's mind. Finally, Azeem bhai
stepped in. 'Baba,' he said, '*abhi nahin baithoge to
zindagi mein phir kabhi nahin baithoge.* (If you don't get
back on her now, you'll never be able to sit on a horse
again.)' He helped Viju mount the horse slowly and
instructed him to keep his legs wide so that Nafrati
couldn't see the crane behind her. Viju did the shot with

*Viju Khote with one leg protruding out, keeping the rifle away
from Nafrati.*

his legs spread-eagled, shivering with fright.

Viju was asked to take part in the riding lessons before the next schedule. Every morning at seven he went from downtown Mumbai to Juhu beach to develop some equestrian skills. When he returned to Bangalore, he discovered that he didn't need to get on the horse again. His next scene was at Gabbar's den, where Kaalia gets killed.

*

The second unit was shooting Hema's tanga sequence when the vehicle went over a stone and skid out of balance. Reshma, the duplicate for Hema, lost her footing and fell in front. The wheel went over her and she fainted. Mohammad Hussain, who was directing the unit, paid her some perfunctory attention and then ordered the next shot to be set up. Azeem bhai, a little taken aback by his matter-of-fact attitude, said, 'Mohammad bhai, *ladki behosh hai* (the girl's fainted).' To which he replied: '*Behosh ho gayi, mari to nahin.* (She's fainted, she hasn't died.)'

Reshma survived that fall with a few scratches, but Hussain didn't. His one line caused enormous tension. The fighters were up in arms. Azeem bhai was equally offended. Shooting came to a halt. Ramesh soon got to hear of the incident. He spoke to both Hussain and Azeem bahi at length, quizzed the stuntmen and eventually decided that it was best to let Hussain go.

Hussain's departure brought a problem into sharper focus. Despite the country's best action experts having been hired, Ramesh wasn't getting what he wanted. He had wanted the look of the Hollywood Western for *Sholay*, and the standards of action teams in India were simply not on par. In brainstorming sessions, an idea slowly began to take shape: Why not get foreign technicians for the action? They might not be able to replicate Hollywood, but it would be a leap into the future for Indian cinema. The decision wasn't easy. Foreign technicians meant new adjustments and additional financial pressure. But making a 70mm

Viju Khote's last scene, at Gabbar's den, where Kaalia gets killed, rescued him from the temperamental mare Nafrati.

adventure with slipshod action made little sense. After all, the motto was No Compromise.

Ajit, who had been living in London for some years now, introduced Ramesh to Michael Samuelson, who ran a firm for equipment hire in London. Samuelson put him in touch with stunt director Jim Allen. Jim was a seasoned professional who had joined films as an apprentice and worked his way up. He had done extensive second unit camera work. One of the projects he had worked on had been shot in Pakistan and he had some idea of what a Hindi film shoot might require. Allen put together a team comprising stunt director Gerry Crampton, stunt co-ordinator Romo Commoro, and a special effects man named John Gant. Gerry, an ex-air force man who had been doing stunts since 1955, had already been to India once, for the shooting of a film called *Tarzan*.

Since neither Jim nor Gerry was a complete stranger to the subcontinent, Ramesh was hopeful that they would quickly acclimatize themselves to the working conditions here. In June 1974, Jim and his team came to Banglalore to assess the requirements and the available facilities. They selected the horses, met the Indian stuntmen, and checked out the equipment and the camera. They also went to see a movie. Ramesh's chief assistant, D. R. Thakkar, took them to see *Haath ki Safai*. Every time a song started, their jaws dropped. They hadn't seen anything like this before. Thakkar was amused by their reaction and told them that *Sholay* would also have a

number of songs, which left the foreign technicians
wondering what they'd got themselves into.

In September the London team joined the unit in
Ramanagaram. Songs, Jim and Gerry discovered, were
the least of their problems. India on a holiday and India
on work were two different worlds. Much of the top crew
spoke English, but accents complicated communication.
Azeem bhai barely managed to string a sentence together
and Paaji's Punjabi inflections flew high over their heads.
And the heat was a horror. In less than a week, Jim's face
was burnt crisp. To prevent dehydration, the doctor
advised him to drink beer. So while others sipped water,
Jim consumed gallons of beer.

Mainstream Hindi cinema has its own set-in-stone
system. Jim couldn't understand why things had to be so
obvious. Why was heroism so in-your-face? Why di
action have to be equally balanced between the tw
heroes? Ramesh patiently explained the rules. Sometime
they understood. Sometimes the response was simply:
won't do it, you're wasting my time. I know you won
use it in the final cut.' But perhaps the biggest hurdle w:
that in India both knowledge and equipment, as far
films were concerned, were primitive. There were i
safety standards. 'Action' was just a bunch of very bra·
men willing to risk their lives for small money. 'Peop
didn't know how to do things,' says Jim. 'It was or
bloody great frustration.'

And yet Jim describes that period as 'the best six (

*Jim, Gerry and Romo—the foreign technicians
for the action sequences.*

seven months' of his life. Over jumps and horses, bullets
and beer, the two sides bonded, though that took time.
Azeem bhai gracefully bowed out, leaving behind his best
men to complete Ramesh's vision. The *Angrez*, as the unit
called them, had brought gadgets and safety equipment
for stuntmen: shoulder, elbow, knee and ankle pads.
They showed the boys new techniques—using boxes to
cushion falls; how to make horses collapse; how to time
high jumps. First the boys were awkward, but once they
realized that the new equipment and techniques made
things safer, they were encouraged to do better work.

Amjad, who was coordinating the second unit, played
an important role. He spoke good English and acted as

interpreter between the Angrez and the action boys. Amjad would begin the second unit work by paraphrasing Winston Churchill's prayer: 'I pray that Jim Allen can take the following shots today,' he would scribble on top of the call sheets. 'He took the mickey out of me,' laughs Jim. It was Amjad who was largely responsible for the smooth functioning of the unit. He was the perfect go-between, and gradually the initial resentment and suspicion were replaced with mutual respect and friendship.

Aziz bhai, the construction manager, was the other bonding agent. He solved most problems with his ingenious contraptions. Jim had a foul temper and sometimes when things didn't work, he'd fling his hat to the ground and say, 'I

Gerry choreographing the guest house fight sequence.

want Aziz bhai.' But it was nothing that Aziz bhai and a whiskey at night couldn't take care of. 'It would be impossible to think of *Sholay* without Aziz,' says Jim.

The stunts were complicated and time-consuming. Each fall and bullet shot required planning. Before every

125

sequence, Jim, Gerry and the action gang would sit with Divecha and Ramesh to work out the shot division. Their standard was the Hollywood western. They couldn't replicate it, but they had to at least come close. With action, it was impossible to do every shot twice. So they shot on 35mm with 70mm markings; the frame would be blown up later.

The attack on Ramgarh was the typical Red-Indians-attacking-village scene from a western. There were several junior artistes—a child caught in the crossfire, a woman screaming, frightened people trapped in a merry-go-round on fire—and there were guns going off almost every second. The attack ended with a frame

*'Amjad acted as interpreter between the Angrez
and the action boys.'*

*The attack on
Ramgarh.*

straight out of *Butch Cassidy and the Sundance Kid*:
Veeru and Jai, crouched side by side, shooting the
baddies. But the scene wasn't just all high-octane action.
It was also equal parts drama. There is a lull in the
shooting and Veeru signals to the Thakur to pick up a
gun, and the Thakur, stone-faced, does nothing. The
sequence leads to the Thakur's tragic story that is the
dramatic crux of the film. So this attack sequence had to
have the right balance of action and emotion to make the
required impact. Despite being choreographed to the last
bullet, the sequence took fifteen days to shoot.

Basanti's chase sequence was equally complicated.
Hema's safety was the prime concern. Most of the shots
were done with a camera vehicle towing the tanga. For

127

some, the camera was placed inside the tanga, but the horses were removed to minimize danger. For the long shots and the scene in which the tanga overturns, a double was used. Between actors, horses, camera arrangements, technical and engineering problems, shooting this sequence took twelve days.

Sometimes the problems weren't technical. Jim wanted all close-ups of the characters firing guns to be done with real bullets. On the screen, blank cartridges would look unmistakably like blanks, besides, they gave off big flames—a discerning eye could easily spot them as fakes. Real bullets added a touch of authenticity. In the climax sequence, just after the '*Jab tak hai jaan*' song, Jai rescues Veeru and Basanti. Veeru, holding a fainting Basanti, was required to kick open a trunk of bullets, grab a handful, load a gun and move on. There was only one problem: Paaji was tipsy.

Dharmendra in action: the attack on Ramgarh.

He had been sipping spiked coconut water all day and was eventually so high that he could not kick the trunk open. As the takes continued, the

128

exasperation increased. Finally, Dharmendra managed to kick the box open, grabbed the bullets, loaded the gun, and, in frustration, fired it. Amitabh was standing on the rock above. The bullet whizzed close past him. Jim threw his hat down in disgust and walked off the set. Later Dharmendra apologized to the unit, and stayed sober for the next few days.

But by the end of the shoot, Dharmendra had won over the Angrez team with his charm and large-heartedness. Gerry often wore a green pea cap, which he said a Hollywood star had given him. Dharmendra asked for it and Gerry gladly parted with his prized possession. The Angrez thought Paaji was a world class star, and he, like the other members of the *Sholay* crew, acknowledged

'Basanti's chase sequence took twelve days.'

129

that the Englishmen had revolutionized Hindi film action, both the way it looked and the way it was done.

*

When asked why he is searching for two petty criminals, the Thakur replies, '*Vo badmash hain, lekin bahadhur hain, katharnak hain isliye ki ladna jante hain, bure hain magar insaan hain.* (They're thugs but they're brave, and dangerous because they know how to fight; they may be crooked but they are human.)' The train sequence was to be visual proof this. It had to be a spectacular event, unmatched in dimension, ambition and adrenalin, with a few human touches thrown in.

Yedekar wandered around Gujarat for two weeks, looking for a suitable location. The train track had to have a rough-hewn, barren look, and it had to be an appropriate spot to make a tunnel and an operational steam engine. He settled on the Panvel-Uran track. It was a one-track line with a train that crossed once in the morning and once in the evening. It seemed perfect. But first, they had to take measurements and make their plans.

It was going to be a complicated shoot with two and sometimes three cameras. The cameras would have to be put on rigs and special contraptions to get everything in frame: the horses, the train, the actors. Trolleys had to be fitted so that one of the cameras could move parallel to the train. To design the right camera-carrying rigs, it was necessary to know the exact topography, down to the last milestone, hillock and boulder, so that the camera wouldn't smash into something. So Anwar and Aziz bhai walked from Panvel to Uran taking measurements. It took three days.

Shooting for the train sequence began in end-February 1975. The only problem was that railway law dictated that two trains could not be on the same track at the same time. So the *Sholay* unit would shoot early in the morning, come back to Panvel and get off the track well before the local train was scheduled to make its morning run. Then they would resume shooting till around 5 p.m. and once again get off when the train made its evening run. Actual working time was reduced to five, perhaps six hours. Obviously it couldn't work like this.

The production staff was dispatched to take care of the problem. Officially the railway bureaucracy could not give permission for two trains to be on the same track at the same time. So they arrived at an 'understanding'. A per-day charge was levied, and the film unit was also told to organize a daily *langar*, a free public meal. Officials in the area brought their families and friends to avail of the free food. Of course the officials weren't the only ones with a grievance. The local farmers, who had a hard enough time with the infertile terrain, now had an

'The train sequence . . . had to be a spectacular event.'

additional train belching burning coal onto their meager crops and starting fires. Another understanding was reached. The langar was thrown open to the farmers too. As news of the shooting and the free food spread, more and more families started showing up. The crowd was almost unmanageable by the time the people from the anti-corruption bureau came.

They were on an official investigation to unravel how two trains were being allowed to run on the track. For a minute, Ramesh thought, 'This could be the end of the road.' But the anti-corruption officials were made to 'understand' too.

Sholay pumped money into the local economy through the months it took to shoot the train sequence. Local people were hired to work on the location, and shops and small businesses in the area sold material to the film crew.

Some residents also used rather unconventional means to make some money. One day, Jim Allen and his crew were driving back from Mumbai, when they approached four young boys herding two cows. The boys spotted a not-to-be-missed opportunity. They drove the cows straight into the car. The next day, the Angrez were not allowed on the sets till Ramesh coughed up a sufficient amount of money for their terrible offence.

Even the local criminals benefited. Every morning, some equipment, or-workers' clothes or shoes would be missing. Soon enough, an enterprising resident opened a shop near by which stocked basic items (the area was notorious for its small-time smugglers, and there was never any dearth of these 'items'). Most mornings, a production boy would head to the shop to replace the materials stolen the night before.

Bending the rules allowed the work to go on, but only just. The unit would reach the location by 7 a.m. but work rarely began before 8 or 8.30 a.m. due to some big or small mishap that had happened during the night. The actual shooting too was incredibly time-consuming. Shot breakdowns and planning had been done extensively, but the paperwork could not have taken into account the endless unknown factors. Coordination was a Herculean task: when the camera was ready, the train wouldn't be in momentum; when the train was in motion, the horses refused to move. A five-second shot would take five hours to film. It was, as Ramesh puts it, 'maddening, maddening, maddening.'

The nature of the sequence was such that unforeseen delays were inevitable. The scenes involving horses, for instance. Special pits had been dug for the horse-falls. They were layered with boxes and camouflaged with earth. A horse would ride into it and automatically buckle. But the shot couldn't be done with the same horse twice, because once a horse knew the pit, it wouldn't ride over it again. Also, given the dangers involved— stuntmen clad in special padding had to jump thirty to forty feet off the moving train—the shooting couldn't really be rushed.

The most dangerous bit was the shot of the speeding train crashing through a barrier of wood logs. It was a three-camera shoot. The train was reversed six kilometres, to be driven into a pile of logs at high speed. One camera was placed near the logs to catch a frontal shot as the train came crashing through. At that speed, anything was possible. Ramesh told Anwar, '*Yaar Anwar, last schedule chal raha hai. Dhyan rakhna.* (It's the last schedule, Anwar, be careful.)' Anwar replied, '*Aap befikar raho.* (Don't you worry.)' Anwar and Aziz bhai did the log arrangement, cutting and fitting, so that they would come down easily. Mushtaq Merchant played the engine driver.

The scene was done after lunch. At the designated time,

'Mushtaq Merchant played the engine driver.'

the train drove into the logs. It was going so fast that the driver was only able to bring it to a halt some four or five kilometres from the site. Afterward, Ramesh announced pack-up. No one had the energy to shoot any more. The train sequence was in the can. It had taken seven weeks to shoot.

*

The *'Mehbooba'* song was a five-day shoot. A set was constructed at R.K. Studios in Chembur. Actor Jalal Agha had been selected to play the gypsy singer opposite Helen. But on the first day, he didn't' show up. He was busy

performing shows out of town. So Ramesh canned
Helen's solo shots and waited, simmering with anger. He
decided that if Jalal did not show up on day two as well,
he would do the part himself. Luckily Jalal reported for
shooting the next morning. He wore knee-pads for his
dance around the fire, but the more gruelling
shots—during which he was required to stay on his knees
for long, vigorous movements—were done by a
professional dancer. Salim dropped in a few times during
the shooting of the song, primarily to see Helen. Their
love story had only just begun; it would make headlines in
a few years.

The final scene to be shot was the one towards the

'The "Mehbooba" song was a five-day shoot.'

The final scene to be shot: the Thakur offers Veeru and Jai the job.

beginning of the film, when the Thakur meets Veeru and Jai outside the jail and offers them the job. And after nearly two years and 450 shifts, *Sholay* was complete.

137

CHAPTER 8

YEH HAATH NAHIN, PHAANSI KA PHANDA HAI

Amjad Khan had a peculiar voice. He wasn't big then—the girth came later—but he had the appearance of a large man; he rarely walked into a room unnoticed. But his voice did not match his hulking presence. It wasn't thin, but it wasn't the rich baritone laced with threat that villains of the day cultivated either. Amjad's voice was both raspy and sing-song. He sounded like a child with a bad cough.

Ramesh loved it. It added to Gabbar's menacing air because it was so unexpected. The voice, like the man, was unpredictable. It was a peculiarity that set him apart. But Salim-Javed weren't so sure. A powerful villain with a small voice could wreck the film. They advised Ramesh to dub Amjad's voice. The suggestion did the rounds and almost immediately many others were saying the same thing: '*Bahut dheeli awaaz hai* (The voice has no punch),' they whispered. Some, like Jaya and Jim, spoke vehemently in favour of Amjad. 'You are totally wrong,' Jim said to Ramesh. 'Do what you want, it's your film, but you would be mad to change his voice.' Ramesh listened to both sides and remained mysteriously silent.

Amjad was shattered. This was his make-or-break movie. He was the underdog in a crowd of stars. Dubbing his voice in such a high-profile project would ruin his career even before it had really taken off. First Salim and Javed had suggested replacing him in the movie, and now this. Amjad had worked extremely hard to overcome his initial nervousness and no one could fault his performance, so why was he still being treated as a liability? The murmurs about his voice being unsuitable for Gabbar seemed to him further proof of the fact that there was something personal in all this. He was completely convinced now that certain people were trying to sabotage his career.

The final decision, of course, had to be Ramesh's. He went with his gut feeling. Amjad would dub for Gabbar himself. But the doubters continued to voice their reservations almost till the day *Sholay* was released. The ultimate irony was that after the release, the voice that almost did not make it to the screen sold thousands of records.

Ramesh had an intimate bonding with his actors; he understood their psychology. His most important attribute was patience. He was unflappable; he rarely panicked or lost his cool. His relaxed attitude helped him to extract exemplary work from his actors, both on and off the sets. And his patience wasn't just reserved for the stars. Even the one-line actors were treated like artists. Viju Khote, while dubbing, couldn't get a line right—instead of 'Aadhi mutthi jawar' he kept saying 'Aadhi mutthi gawar'. Ramesh just asked him to take a break. Viju stepped out of the dubbing theatre for a few minutes, had a cup of tea and finally got the twentieth take right.

*

The hardest part was the editing for the final cut. Ramesh spent hours sitting at the editing table with his editor, Madhav Rao Shinde, affectionately called Dada, who could be easily spotted in a crowd by his thick curly white hair and his red, pan-stained mouth. Through the months of shooting, Shinde had been editing Sholay at Mumbai's Film Centre. Rushes would be flown in from Bangalore, Shinde would edit, and then the rough cut would be flown back to Bangalore for Ramesh's approval. Shinde had also spent a month in Bangalore, but very little work had got done because on most days Ramesh was too exhausted after shooting to pay much attention to editing. So Shinde would sit with Jim on the action sequences, but here again progress was slow. The two would squabble over each cut and there were frequent heated arguments—Jim protected his work like a lioness her cubs.

Shinde had a gargantuan task. Salim-Javed's script was brilliant, and so many of the cuts were suggested by the script itself, but the film was simply too long. Ramesh had exposed over 300,000 feet of negative. It had to be whittled down to less than 20,000 feet. Shinde had edited all of Ramesh's films and by now had an instinctive feel for what Ramesh wanted. But he had never had so much material to work with.

Entire sequences ended up on the Film Centre floor. Among the best that didn't make it was a comedy sequence that preceded the Soorma Bhopali section. Maruti, a popular comedian of the day, played a dhaba owner in it. Veeru and Jai eat at the dhaba, gargle and spit

The dhaba sequence that never made it to the final cut.

vigorously, and have a fight with Maruti when he objects to their doing *quli* in his premises. Mushtaq Merchant playing an eccentric Parsi gentleman had a scene in which Veeru and Jai steal his motorcycle. He was reduced to a figure ebbing into the horizon just before the '*Yeh dosti*' song. Sachin's death scene was also cut. Shinde kept the brutal lines of dialogue out, slicing from Gabbar killing an ant to the horse carrying Ahmed's dead body into the village. The edit fit with the overall tone of the film, in which violence is more often suggested than seen. The audience never sees Thakur's arms being hacked off. Like the cut from Gabbar raising the sword to an armless Thakur, Ahmed's unseen death had far greater impact.

The final edit took a month. Every morning, Ramesh arrived at Film Centre at noon and stayed there till after sundown. The first cut was approximately 21,000 feet long, nearly four hours of film. It was also grisly. There was too much blood. A meeting was convened and it was decided that the violence would have to be toned down. Shinde then excised most of the bloody scenes. Despite all the violence in *Sholay*, blood makes only guest appearances.

The final censored film was 18,000 feet. At three hours and twenty minutes, it was still long enough to throw show timings off.

*

Most producers are washed out as they move into post-production. The budget is spent, the release date looms large, and the attitude is: let's quickly finish the film and recover our investment. But the Sippys were patient, and still as committed to making a quality film as they had been at the beginning. *Sholay*'s budget was nearing an unprecedented three crores of rupees. It was madness, the industry pundits said. Even at Rs 22.5 lakh per territory, recovering the mammoth budget seemed impossible. Yet the Sippys continued to spend. Ramesh was convinced that every technical level added a dimension to the film, and he worked on every cut and sound.

The background music alone took a month. In the 1970s, background music was composed, not sampled from already existing tracks. Ramesh gave Pancham a free hand, his only brief being that the score should have a symphonic feel. Ramesh imagined soaring music that underlined the epic ambience of the film. But he also wanted unique sounds. He wanted signature tunes that evoked character. He wanted Gabbar's menace and Radha's tragic serenity to translate into sounds so distinctive that even when the character wasn't on screen, just the note would suggest his or her presence.

Pancham rarely created in the studio. First, he and Ramesh would decide which scenes required music and what it should be. Pancham's assistants, Dipan and Santosh, took furious notes during the discussions and

143

made the markings. Once the essentials had been decided upon, extensive research was done to determine what combination of existing or improvised musical instruments would give the desired sounds. For Gabbar's high-pitch screeching theme, a homegrown instrument was used. It was a brass pot with a one-and-a-half-inch tube in the centre, surrounded by smaller half- and quarter-inch tubes. When water was poured into the central tube, a high-pitched sound emanated from the smallest tubes and a low-pitched sound from the bigger ones. The only problem was that the instrument made a different sound each time. About fifteen takes were recorded before Pancham heard a sound he liked. They made a loop and used the same sound each time. The brass-pot note was married with a cello, and Gabbar's distinctive theme was ready, an entirely new sound for the industry.

The influence of the western was quite pronounced even in the background score. The title music started with a French horn, segued into the strains of the taar shehnai for a rustic touch, and went back to the French horn. But the team also experimented. For Basanti's tanga chase sequence, Pancham wanted only a tabla. Many musicians thought it was too spare. But Pancham knew that a single tabla sound would enhance the frenzied chase more than an entire orchestra. Pandit Shamta Prasad played the tabla for the scene. Pancham played the mouth organ for Jai himself. He also flipped the coin for the coin sounds.

Amjad was the only actor who sat in on the background recordings, everyone else was too busy. *Sholay* was all Amjad had. One day, the assistants took him aside and asked him to play a prank on the dholak player, Devi. Devi had been clowning around, imitating Amjad's '*Arre o Sambha*' line. Amjad put on his best menacing look and approached Devi. He did not touch the man, only leaned close and growled, 'Don't. Imitate. Me.' Intimidated by the looming figure and the unsettling voice, Devi turned pale and nodded. And then he ran out of the recording theatre. He had just given up cigarettes, but he headed straight for Pancham's car, pulled out his pack and started smoking.

The last scene—Veeru and Basanti meeting in the train—was shot after the background music was done, so Pancham had to create music for the scene without seeing it. But it wasn't difficult. The long gestation hadn't dulled Ramesh's enthusiasm, he lived the film, every frame of it. He gave Pancham a detailed breakdown of what he was going to shoot, including how many shots the scene would have and from whose point of view it would be, and how many seconds each shot would be. When the shot was actually done, the music was out of synch by only a few frames.

The Sippys had decided early on that a 70mm format would have to have stereophonic sound. Epic visuals without equally impressive sound would be like a half-baked pudding. Each note in the film had to match the grand camerawork. Throughout, Ramesh had planned his shots keeping stereophonic perspectives in mind. What the Sippys didn't realize was that stereophonic sound meant shifting operations to London. There wasn't a studio in India that could handle a stereophonic mix.

Jim Allen made inquiries. He found Twickenham Studio, which was located in a London suburb. First Twickenham sent a sound engineer to Mumbai. He saw the film, made notes and gave instructions on how sounds should be recorded. Every sound—the movement of the carriage (the original tanga was brought into the studio for the recording), a bell ringing, the train approaching—was recorded on a separate track. Ramesh carried all the sounds he needed from Mumbai to London. Everything, except the bullet sound effects and 'dishoom-dishoom'. Fight sound effects in Mumbai were generic; whether it was a fall or a blow or a punch, everything sounded the same. And so, only the fight sounds were created in London, the rest were recorded in Mumbai and carried to Twickenham. For three months, Ramesh went back and forth between London and Mumbai, mixing sounds, before the last bit of work on the film was completed to his satisfaction.

Sholay was finally ready in July. Two and a half years of labour lay spooled in tins. Looking at the film, Ramesh thought he had turned the curve, that the hardest part was behind him. He did not know that the battle had just begun.

*

Gabbar Singh dies in *Sholay*. Or at least he does in the original *Sholay* that Ramesh had shot, that Salim-Javed had written. The Thakur kills Gabbar with his feet, wearing shoes that the servant Ramlal has fashioned with nails fitted in the soles. The armless Thakur first crushes Gabbar's arms. Then they stand face to face, two armless warriors, two equals. And then the Thakur pounds Gabbar to death as if he were a venomous snake; he does not stop till the dacoit is a bloody mess under his shoes. Then he breaks down and cries. He weeps long and hard:

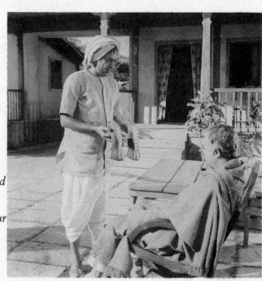

Ramlal fashioned the shoes with which the Thakur kills Gabbar in the original Sholay.

his life's mission is complete, but all he feels is a vast emptiness. It is a pyrrhic victory. Revenge begets only loss.

The Central Board of Film Censors hated this ending. The Board had a written-in-stone set of rules, and with a state of Emergency having been declared in the country, its powers to dictate and control what was shown on screen had multiplied. The Board objected to the suggestion that a police officer—even one who was no longer in service—would take the law into his own hands and commit a murder. They also objected to the film's balletic violence. It wasn't graphic, but it was so finely choreographed that it had far greater impact than actual gore. The audience wouldn't see Thakur's arms being chopped off, but the visual cut from Gabbar raising the sword to the Thakur standing with his empty shirtsleeves flapping in the wind was unforgettable. Ramesh had made violence aesthetic and attractive. If passed, *Sholay* would open the floodgates for lesser filmmakers. There would be cuts in *Sholay*. But first, the Sippys would have to change the end.

Ramesh was incensed. It was almost as though he was being penalized for being talented. Every nuance in the film had been carefully considered and crafted. Not a frame was superfluous. The Board wasn't just asking for cuts, it was asking for a totally different conclusion—an ending that would have the police intervening at the crucial moment to prevent the Thakur from killing

Gabbar. It seemed like a parody of what had been done in a hundred other films. It had none of the bleakness or tragedy of the original. With a conclusion so feeble, *Sholay* would no longer be Ramesh's vision. It would become another film altogether.

In the resolutely repressive environment of the Emergency, fundamental rights did not exist. Neither did artistic freedom. Compromise wasn't a choice, it was the only option. But Ramesh was adamant. He hadn't toiled for two years to cop out now. He wasn't going to change the end.

There was a flurry of meetings with various levels of the Board. Ramesh tried to reason with the members of the Board, pointing out to them the flaws in their own argument: the ending they wanted—an inspector and constables arriving in the nick of time at Gabbar's den—would make the police force look foolish. After all, where had this fearless police force been through the film when the dacoit was murdering and pillaging villages? Besides, it threw off the whole shape of the film and made it seem ridiculous; it made a mockery of Sanjeev Kumar's carefully nuanced and understated performance, which was constructed precisely to lead to the final explosive epiphany. They were trampling on an artist's creativity. But the Board would not budge. Increasingly frustrated, at a few meetings Ramesh did something most uncharacteristic of him—he raised his voice.

The Sippys called on every connection they had. G. P.

Sippy was a resourceful man with considerable clout. He worked the phone for hours, arranging high-powered meetings. Anyone who might have influenced the Board got a call. Father and son also had bitter rows. Ramesh argued as an artist who was watching his work being mauled, and G. P. as a realist who knew that compromise was inevitable. At one point, Ramesh even considered taking his name off the film. After all, he says, 'who was going to explain to the discerning audiences that actually this was what was intended but this was what had come out, and why it had happened?' But eventually the producer prevailed. G. P. explained ground reality to Ramesh: If they were stubborn, the film wouldn't get released. Being a lawyer himself, he knew better than anyone else the futility of going to court. In an Emergency, they had no rights. And at the end of three years of production, they had very little money. They couldn't afford to take the higher moral ground.

The release date had been fixed for 15 August 1975. As was the practice then, Polydor had released the music two months earlier. In an extraordinary display of confidence, they had released 30,000 records, double the usual film launch. They had also offered the dealers a special scheme. At the end of the year, dealers could traditionally return 7.5 per cent of the goods that they had not managed to sell. Polydor told the dealers: Take as many records of *Sholay* as you want, but return the unsold ones before the film's release. After the release, if the music ran and dealers wanted records, they would have to pay more. Any delay in release would adversely affect Polydor's business. There really was no option; Ramesh would have to re-shoot the end.

It was a Herculean task. It was already 20 July. Within the following week the ending would have to be re-shot and re-dubbed, the background music redone and remixed in London, and then the film printed for release. The cast was hastily summoned. Sanjeev Kumar was attending a film festival in the Soviet Union. He flew to India immediately. For two days, the cast and crew assembled in Ramanagaram. It seemed like old times again. They were back amidst the giant boulders, in the harsh sunlight, all committed as before to the ambitious project that had brought them together.

The censors also excised some of the violence in other parts of the film. One important scene that was hacked was of Ramlal, with a determined look on his face, driving vicious-looking nails into the soles of the shoes which he would then take to the Thakur, and with which the Thakur would kill Gabbar. With the cuts implemented and the new ending inserted, the Board of Film Censors was satisfied, and the final 70mm prints were then made in London. The negative for the 35mm was brought back to Mumbai and printed at Film Centre. And so *Sholay* was ready for release—a weaker version of *Sholay*, with a new, lesser ending.

But apparently, somewhere in this world, rumoured to

151

'A publicity blitz announced the coming of Sholay.'

be impossible to trace now, a few prints survive of the original, untouched film, with all its final bleakness intact. Occasionally, videotapes and DVDs of this original film surface, copied from copies of copies. Those who have seen these nth-generation copies say that despite the fuzziness and the bad sound, the Thakur's hopeless weeping is chilling, and it becomes clear to the viewer that all the visceral attractions of power and violence lead inevitably to this agony, this loss. In those long-ago days of the seventies, this was the moral vision that Ramesh Sippy and Salim-Javed tried to bring to the Indian viewer. Due to the wisdom of our censors, what we got instead was an easy pabulum about the virtues of following the law, and a film that at least in part had an aesthetic clumsiness forced onto it.

*

A publicity blitz announced the coming of *Sholay*. For the first time, huge hoardings at Chowpatty Beach were used to advertise a film. The hoardings, a collage of the principal characters, had been designed by a publicist called C. Mohan. The posters announced: 'The greatest film ever made' and 'The greatest story ever told'. Often at night Amjad and Shaila would drive to Chowpatty, park their car and stare at the posters. Shaila loved seeing Amjad's face, giant, impassive, already famous.

Ramesh was in a daze as the release date approached.

He and Anwar were checking prints at Film Centre, but he wasn't actually watching the film. He was just seeing bits and pieces, never the whole. G. P. Sippy had seen the entire film in London. He was supremely confident about his product. His son had surpassed himself. Every last paisa spent showed on screen: *Sholay* was a masterful combination of commerce and art. A few weeks before the release, G. P. was heading for his favourite haunt, the derby, with his son Vijay and his Bangalore distributor, Suresh Malhotra. Suresh asked, 'Sippy saab, *kaisi lagi aapko picture?* (How did you like the picture?) Sippy replied, '*Yeh picture dus saal nahin utregi.* (This film will run for ten years.)'

There wasn't time for trials. But some of the cast had seen a rush print in Bangalore during the climax re-shoot. At the end of the show, Macmohan, who plays Sambha, was in tears. They had been drinking a little and everyone thought Mac had become sentimental. '*Kya hua*, Mac?' they asked laughing. '*Paagal ho gaya kya, picture itni achhi lagi ki ro raha hai?* (What's the matter, Mac? Do you like the film so much that it makes you cry?)' Mac was quiet. But as they exited the theatre, he asked Ramesh, 'Rameshji, how could this happen? I've become an extra in the film. Just edit me out. I don't want it.' Ramesh replied, 'Mac, *jitna main kaat sakta tha, maine kaata. Jitna censor kaat sakta tha, censor ne kaata. Ab kuchh nahin ho sakta.* (Mac, I've edited as much as I could, and then the censors did their bit. There's nothing

'Sambha is perhaps the only character in cinema to be immortalized by just three words: "Poore pachaas hazaar."'

I can do now.) But I will tell you one thing. If this picture runs, nobody will forget Sambha.'

His words proved prophetic. Sambha is perhaps the only character in cinema to be immortalized by just three words: *'Poore pachaas hazar.'*

CHAPTER 9

IS STORY MAIN EMOTION HAI, DRAMA HAI, TRAGEDY HAI

Sholay flopped. The critics were harsh, the performance at the box office was mixed, and the industry, waiting for the smallest hint to knock the mega project of the brash young director, was merciless. For the first time since Salim-Javed narrated the four-line idea two and a half years ago, Ramesh panicked.

The weeks leading up to the release had been a blur. Ramesh was bug-eyed from lack of sleep. The climax re-shoot and remix had increased the birth pangs ten-fold. Prints and negatives were flying between Mumbai and London. There was no time to savour the finished product. Meanwhile the hype had assumed a life of its own. The trade could talk of little else. Every day there was a new rumour: the film was being offered an 'Adults only' certificate; the censor board wanted further cuts; the 70mm prints were not ready, so the Sippys were postponing the release date . . . and on and on. A column in *Trade Guide*, the industry trade magazine, wrote: 'Wherever we went, we heard nothing but *Sholay* . . . sometimes we also thought we would get allergic to it. Everyone wanted to see nothing but *Sholay*. Many people in the industry preferred to discuss *Sholay* to their own films.'

Minerva, on Mumbai's Lamington Road, had been selected as *Sholay's* main theatre. Minerva was known by its tag line: 'The pride of Maharashtra.' It was the only theatre at the time with a screen big enough for 70mm and six-track sound, and with 1500 seats it was also the largest cinema in the country. The theatre was dressed up like a bride for the release. Outside stood 30-foot cutouts of the star cast: Dharmendra, Amitabh, Sanjeev, Hema, Jaya and, of course, Amjad Khan. Inside were rows of photographs from the film, and garlands of flowers.

The premiere night was a glittering affair. On 14 August, two premieres were held simultaneously, one at Minerva and one at Excelsior. For the cast and crew, it felt like life had come full circle. It was pouring outside, just as it had been on the first day of the shoot, and Jaya was glowing again—this time pregnant with Abhishek. The industry's top names, all spiffed up and shiny, walked into Minerva to see what the fuss was all about. But there was a problem—the 70mm print hadn't arrived yet. It was still stuck at the customs.

The 70mm saga was a plot worthy of Salim-Javed. A

senior bureaucrat in the finance ministry had declared war on the Sippys. Since a large part of the post-production work was done in London, several permissions were sought. The bureaucrat felt he hadn't been given adequate importance and was still simmering. He decided to use every ploy to throw *Sholay* off track.

When the unit went to London, he wrote to the Indian High Commission there to keep close tabs on them. The Commission obliged. When the first 70mm print came out, Ramesh decided to have a screening for friends and family. It was fixed for 10 one morning at the Odeon at Marble Arch. Ramesh also rang up the High Commissioner. 'But how,' said a senior secretary at the Commission, 'can you have a screening? You don't have permission for that. Your contract says materials must go straight from Technicolour to India.' Then suddenly the secretary changed tack: 'Okay, we'll come.' Ramesh had an intuition that all wasn't well and at the last minute cancelled the screening. It was fortunate. Because at exactly 9:50, people from the High Commission turned up to seize the print.

Orders were sent out to stall the Sippys at every level. When Ramesh landed in Mumbai, he was strip-searched. When even that didn't produce anything, the bureaucrat simply told the custom officials not to clear the print. On the morning of 14 August the prints were still lying in tins at the customs.

G. P. Sippy, never a man to take a beating lying down,

went into action. He organized a high-level meeting. Attending on G. P.'s terrace were Rajni Patel, a noted lawyer and a close confidant of Prime Minister Indira Gandhi, and V. C. Shukla, minister for Information and Broadcasting, who was also to be the chief guest at the premiere. Shukla simply called Delhi and blasted into the bureaucrat: 'What are you trying to do? Tell them to release the prints *now*.' The bureaucrat, taken aback by the reach of the Sippys, mumbled a quick 'Yes sir.' But he managed to delay the prints by a few more hours. By the evening they still hadn't reached the theatre, so *Sholay's* premiere audience saw a 35mm print.

Through the screening, there was little reaction. The audience seemed unmoved. There was no laughter, no tears, no applause. Just silence. 'It was scary,' recalls Geeta. In the stalls sat Prakash Mehra, who had once been one of the contenders for the four-line story. '*Maine yeh kahani kyun chhod di?* (Why did I let this story go?)' he asked himself aloud. After the film, as the audience streamed out of the hall, Pancham, who had been sitting next to Mehra, whispered to him: '*Log toh gaaliyan de rahen hain.* (But the people here seem to hate it.)' 'Don't worry,' Prakash replied, 'this film is a hit. No one can stop it.'

The missing 70mm print arrived after the screening and the *Sholay* crew decided to see it. After all, this was what they had sweated for. Around one in the morning, when most of the invitees had left, the film was screened

159

again. Through the screening the Sippy production staff plied the audience with drinks. By the time the film finished at 5 a.m., many were inebriated. Salim had been drinking and simmering for much of the evening. During the interval, he had gone up to Amjad to congratulate him but the actor, still smarting from the voice controversy, had turned away.

After the screening Amjad was sitting on the Minerva steps. As people exited, Salim walked up to him and loudly demanded to know what his problem was. The argument quickly grew loud and aggressive. Director Ramesh Behl, who was standing close by, tried to douse the fire. 'This isn't the time for fights,' he said. A crowd gathered and separated the two warring parties. Amjad was clearly incensed but he did not continue the argument, he just walked away.

The following morning, the feedback ranged from ecstatic to abrasive. Dilip Kumar loved the film, though after the train sequence, he did worry a little: after all, if a film started on such a high note, where would it go from there? Raj Kapoor thought it was 'nice' but could have done with a little more romance. Rajendra Kumar was more sceptical. There was no mother figure; and what kind of friendship did the two men share?— Jai betrays his friend when he talks to mausi about marrying Basanti to Veeru!

The rest of the film industry wasn't as polite as Kumar. The morning-after-the-premiere grapevine dripped poison. The film was dubbed '*Chholey*', and the main cast, '*Teen maharathi aur ek chooha* (Three warriors and a mouse)'. Everything was wrong with the film. Why would women and family audiences want to see so much gore? The friendship was in such bad taste. Amjad had no presence, and no voice... '*Hindustaniyon ko aisi picturein nahin achhi lagti hain* (Indians don't like films like this),' pronounced a prominent industry figure.

The critics agreed. Taking off on the title of the film, K. L. Amladi writing in *India Today* called it a 'dead ember'. 'Thematically, it's a gravely flawed attempt,' he wrote. *Filmfare*'s Bikram Singh wrote: 'The major trouble with the film is the unsuccessful transplantation it attempts—grafting a western on the Indian milieu. The film remains imitation western—neither here nor there.' The trade magazines weren't gushing either. 'The classes and families will find no reason for a repeat show,' said *Film Information. Trade Guide* called it a milestone but qualified the praise with a negative comparison with *Deewaar.*

Now it was up to the audience. On 15 August 1975, *Sholay* was released in the Bombay territory with forty prints.

*

Despite the notorious Mumbai *ki barish* which was coming down in torrents, the crowds turned up; in fact,

many people had started queuing up outside the theatres
the night before the advance booking opened. Amidst the
eager first-day audience roamed the police, keeping order
and a check on the black marketeers. At least in one
theatre they found that the owner himself had held back
over a thousand tickets. The demand for tickets was so
high that in some theatres the managers just put the phone
off the hook. Looking at the advance, trade pundits were
predicting that the film would cross a business of eleven
lakh rupees in its first week.

But the buoyancy was balanced by the legions of
cynics. After the premiere, the critics and industrywalas
had already given their verdict, and there had been more

'People had started queuing up outside the theatres the night
before the advance booking opened.'

brickbats than bouquets. Even the black marketeers—
those most knowledgeable of critics—were a little
apprehensive about the film. Sure, it was the Midas-touch
team of the Sippys and Salim-Javed, and yes, the film had
an impressive star cast, but the story sounded strange:
Sanjeev was playing a handicapped man and Jaya a silent
widow, and there was some new villain who wasn't in the
mould of the suave smugglers of the day like Ajit and
Pran. In fact, some blackies were dismissing *Sholay* as a
second-rate take-off on *Mera Gaon Mera Desh*, which
had made tonnes of money for them earlier.

The Sippys' only hope was that the audience would
prove them all wrong.

*

There was no reaction. On Friday, 15 August, the first
day of *Sholay*'s release, Ramesh drove from one theatre to
another to assess the reaction of the audience. As on the
premiere night, there was only silence. Over the weekend,
panic set in. The theatres were full but the reports were
mixed. Pundits were now predicting disaster. No one told
Ramesh that, but he could see it in the faces of all those he
met. Every one wore that peculiar expression of pity and
awkwardness. They met him like he was a man in
mourning.

The Sippys moved into damage-control mode. On the
weekend, a hurried meeting was convened at Amitabh's

house. G. P. Sippy, Ramesh and Amitabh put their heads together to try and come up with solutions. Since there was no fear of piracy at the time, the release of the film in the major territories was being staggered. They could make substantial alterations before *Sholay* hit the rest of the country. One suggestion was re-shooting the end yet again. Amitabh, post *Zanjeer* and *Deewar*, was too big a star to die. Jai was just a petty thief, he hadn't done anything to deserve death. Perhaps an ending in which the two couples walk into the sunset would salvage the film.

Salim-Javed were vehement that the film shouldn't be touched. Ramesh considered the suggestion for a new ending, but not for long. His head said he should do it but his heart wouldn't allow it. He went with his heart. A happy end would compromise his film even further. It was important that the audience leave the theatre with a feeling that something had been left unfinished. That slight ache in the heart was part of the film's appeal. Not a frame would be touched. He would swim or sink with the film.

As the week wore on the anxiety of the crew turned into depression. On Monday morning, when the second week advance booking opened, there were modest queues outside Minerva and Excelsior where the 70mm prints were showing. At the other theatres, hardly two or three people stood for tickets. In most of the suburban theatres, matinee shows had less than fifty per cent collections. For Ramesh, this was confirmation that all was lost. He was devastated. That evening he walked into Film Centre, where more prints were being made, and told Anwar, '*Printing band kar do. Abhi kuchh samajh main nahin aa raha hai* (Stop the printing. I don't understand what's going on.)' At home, the unflappable demeanour cracked. It was the first time in his remarkable career that he was facing a flop. 'I think I've failed,' he told Geeta.

At the Sippy house the tension was palpable. G. P. Sippy stood rock-steady and characteristically optimistic. He was sure that the film would turn around. But at the back of his mind sat unpleasant thoughts: The film had gone way over budget and creditors had to be paid back. They might never be able to make a film again. This was one gamble

'*One suggestion was re-shooting the end yet again. Amitabh, post Zanjeer and Deewar, was too big a star to die.*'

that could set them back by years. There were even rumours that the Sippys were packing up and leaving the country.

One week later, on 22 August 1975, *Sholay* was released in Bangalore in six theatres. Suresh Malhotra, the distributor, organized a grand premiere. The entire main cast and crew flew in for the night. Suresh loved *Sholay*. When interviewed by *Film Information* in July, he had predicted that the film would do a business of one crore. But it didn't look like the business would bear his claim. Even before the first week was over, collections took a dip in Bangalore. In the second week, Ramesh called Suresh: 'Look,' he said, 'other distributors are suggesting trimming the film. Do you want any cuts?' 'No,' Suresh told him, 'I won't touch an inch.'

Amitabh was shooting in Kashmir for Yash Chopra's *Kabhi Kabhi*. His co-star, Shashi Kapoor, had seen *Sholay* at Minerva with his children and was convinced that the film was a hit. All of them, including his driver, had enjoyed it. The audience seemed to be having a good time too. But a morose Amitabh insisted that the film had flopped. He literally cried on Shashi's shoulder, '*Nahin yaar, gayi, picture flop ho gayi*. (No, yaar, it's over, the film's a flop.)' Ramesh Sippy has ruined your life, Amitabh's other producers told him. 'After the fabulous shooting,' Amitabh says, 'that felt like a bucket of cold water.' Back in Mumbai, Jaya was equally upset. *Sholay* wasn't just another film that Amitabh and she had worked in together. They had been personally and emotionally involved with it.

But perhaps the worst affected was Amjad. As the negative feedback filtered in, Amjad became more and more silent. The normally effusive and volatile man retreated into a shell. His house was enveloped in gloom. An equally disheartened Asrani visited him in the first week. Asrani had been shooting at the nearby Mehboob Studio with Aruna Irani and she had suggested dropping in at Amjad's. '*Maine dam laga diya, ab nahi chali. Kya kar sakte hain* (I gave it all I had, but it hasn't worked. There's nothing to be done now),' Amjad told them mournfully. '*Lekin aapki taareef to bahut ho rahi hai* (But there are great things being said about your performance),' Asrani countered. Praise was little consolation. 'What's the use, yaar?' Amjad replied, fighting back tears. 'Salim-Javed have told Ramesh that my voice ruined the picture. Sorry folks, I've missed the bus.'

Trade Guide *wrote, 'The short role of Jaya Bhaduri (also Hema) has not been appreciated . . .'*

167

The trade papers added salt to the smarting wounds. The 23 August *Trade Guide* carried a front-page article titled 'Valuation: *Sholay*'. The article calculated the total cost per major circuit to be Rs 32,70,000 and concluded, '*Sholay* will be a sad experience for distributors . . . Particularly the death of Amitabh and the short role of Jaya Bhaduri (also of Hema) have not been appreciated . . . the industry in general and the production sector in particular have to take a bitter lesson from this issue.' Other articles in the magazine reported that the film 'could have been made with less funds and with better results by a more competent director.' 'One will never know why so much time, effort and valuable foreign exchange was wasted on 70mm,' one article said. '*Sholay* will teach the producer and other moviemakers what to do and what not to do when making exceptionally ambitious films.'

In all the sound and fury, Salim-Javed stood firm. 'Nothing doing,' they said to re-shooting proposals. 'This film will run.' It was the cockiness of youth and the confidence of a job well done. The following week, the two put an advertisement in the trade papers. The ad said that Salim-Javed predict that *Sholay* will 'be a grosser of rupees one crore in each major territory of India.' The trade sniggered. Going by the response, the Sippys would be lucky if *Sholay* managed forty lakh per territory.

*

Salim-Javed were wrong. As it turned out, one crore was a conservative estimate. Mid-week, a curious thing happened: there was little advance booking, but the theatres were full. The proprietor at Geeta cinema in Worli told Ramesh, 'Don't worry, your film is a hit.' It was the first time Ramesh had heard the word used in connection with his film. 'How can you say that?' he asked. 'Because the sales of my soft drinks and ice creams are going down,' the man replied. 'By the interval the audience are so stunned that they are not coming out of the theatre.' Finally Ramesh understood why there was no reaction. People were overawed by what they were seeing. They needed time. Now, clearly, *Sholay* had found its audience.

Word of mouth spread like a juicy rumour. The visuals were epic and the sound was a miracle; when Veeru threw the coin in the climax, people in the 70mm theatres dove under the seats to see where it had fallen. By the third week, the audience was repeating dialogues. It meant that at least some were coming in to see the film for the second time. Polydor noticed this and was quick to act. Record sales weren't good and the music company was in a panic. *Sholay* was its biggest deal ever and only forty per cent of the investment had been recovered so far. Even though people came out of the theatres with smiles on their faces, they didn't buy the music. Polydor even set up special stalls at the theatres, offering discounts, but the audience didn't seem to notice.

The music men were bewildered. What was the problem here? Some key managers were dispatched to the theatres to see the film with the audience. They realized that the reaction to the dialogue was extraordinary. Obviously *Sholay's* visuals and dialogue were so overpowering that the music barely registered. If Polydor wanted to sell more records, it would have to give the audience what they remembered when they left the theatre: the dialogue. About a month after *Sholay* hit the screens, Polydor released a fifty-eight-minute record of selected dialogue. Gabbar Singh featured prominently. The marketing men felt that he made the biggest impact.

The strategy succeeded. Polydor couldn't keep up with the demand as records flew off the shelves. One batch wasn't up to mark technically, so Polydor held it back, but dealers demanded that the records be released, and

The cover of the platinum three-record set of the complete dialogues and songs of Sholay.

even these faulty records got absorbed.

The tide had turned. *Sholay* was beginning to prove all the doomsayers wrong. The trade pundits tried to shift ground without looking stupid. The 6 September 1975 *Trade Guide* issue declared sagely that '*Sholay* is a safe proposition.' But, it asked, 'is this enough?' The editorial titled 'Valuation:

'*Polydor sold over 500,000 records and cassettes.*'

Sholay III' read: '*Sholay* ought to have been another *Bobby* or *Roti Kapada aur Makaan* or *Deewar*. But, unfortunately, it is not.'

As the film caught on, tickets became priceless. The lines at Minerva stretched for a few kilometres, from the theatre to the nearby Tardeo bridge. The bus stop outside was renamed '*Sholay* stop'. The Minerva manager, Sushil Mehra, could barely keep up with the demand. He stayed at the booking window from 8 a.m. to 8 p.m. and finally just moved his family into a two-room apartment at the theatre; going home seemed pointless.

In Bangalore, a special bus plied from Ramnagaram to

171

the theatre that was showing *Sholay*. Every villager, down to the last child, wanted to see the film. It was, in a way, their film as well. An enterprising bus operator started offering a combination—a bus ticket and a *Sholay* ticket for a special price. That way people wouldn't make the long journey only to find that the theatre houseful. The scheme was a sell-out.

Meanwhile, the black marketeers were raking in the moolah. The fifteen-rupee balcony ticket was selling for Rs 200. It was the first time in movie history that tickets had sold for more than Rs 100. Even the incessant rain couldn't keep the audience away. One week Minerva was water-logged, there was four feet of water in the lobby, and still the audience thronged the theatre. Everyone just took off their shoes, rolled up their trousers, waded through the water and got into the theatre. The board outside declared: Houseful. By now, watching *Sholay* in the theatre had become a little like a Karaoke experience. The entire audience would be mouthing the dialogue with the characters. Some had even memorized the sound effects, down to the last flipped-coin sound.

Macmohan hadn't gone to the premiere. He was so upset with his edited blink-and-you-miss-him appearance that he had decided not to see the film. But he couldn't escape *Sholay*. As the weeks passed, he noticed that people on the road were calling him Sambha and asking for autographs. He wondered how this could be? Had Ramesh added a few more lines? He decided to see the film. It was end-September when he walked into Minerva with his family for the evening six o'clock show. It was houseful. In the interval, Mac got mobbed in the balcony. And the audience in the front stalls were shouting for him. When the commotion became too loud, the manager asked Macmohan to show his face. Macmohan obliged.

But it didn't end there. When the audience for the next show found out that Macmohan was in the theatre, they gathered in the lobby, shouting 'Sambha, Sambha.' The police had to be summoned. Finally, the manager had no option: he drove Mac's car to the back entrance and asked him to leave. 'I was totally shocked,' remembers Macmohan. '*Kabhi soch hi nahin sakte the.* (I could never have imagined it.)'

The Sippys stopped listening to the trade. As the collections mounted, it became obvious that they were looking at something big. In September, Ramesh left for London to take his much-deserved holiday. But every week the collections were given to him over the phone. Ten weeks after its release the film was declared a super hit, and on 11 October 1975 *Sholay,* already a blockbuster, was released in the territories of Delhi-U.P., Bengal, the Central Provinces and Hyderabad to a record-breaking box office.

*

Two versions of *Sholay* ran in the country. The Rajshris

were nervous about the length of the film—it ran for three hours twenty minutes and re-configured show timings. The final show ran till well past 12 a.m., but theatres had to shut down at midnight because of the Emergency. So the Rajshris asked Ramesh to clip the film for their territories—essentially Delhi-U.P, Punjab, Rajasthan and the Central Provinces. Initially Ramesh was adamant that his vision remain whole, but after some arm-twisting he agreed to excise the jailer and Soorma Bhopali comedy tracks. They were the only two portions which were unrelated to the rest of the film. So while audiences in the Bombay territory, Bengal and the South saw the whole film, the rest saw a truncated version. But only for eight weeks.

As the queues got longer, it became obvious that show timings weren't going to stop anyone from coming to see the film. So all the scenes were restored and the audience now returned to see the new characters. There were people who had seen the film ten or twelve times already. To the crew's surprise, Gabbar Singh became a phenomenon. The Thakur, Veeru, Jai, Basanti—they were all memorable. But Gabbar loomed larger. The audience had a love-hate relationship with him. Gabbar was genuinely frightening but also widely popular. By now, Polydor had released fifteen dialogue EP's—*Veeru ki Sagai, Hame Jail Jana Hai, Soorma Bhopali, Radha ki Kahani* and, of course, *Gabbar Singh*. Gabbar was the biggest. His lines played in homes across the country and little children imitated his lilting sing-song voice. Soon, Gabbar Singh was selling biscuits.

Sunil Alagh, then group product manager of Britannia, was spending a quiet evening with his wife, Maya, when she suggested that Gabbar would make an excellent advertising icon. At the time, Parle-G was the king of the glucose biscuit market, with a ninety per cent market share. Glucose-D was a minnow with a negligible presence. Sunil jumped at the idea. The connection between Gabbar and Glucose was obvious and path-breaking: children loved Gabbar, they would love

the biscuits he endorsed. He would have the kids literally eating out of the palm of his hand.

Not everyone at Britannia was sold on the concept. Companies used film stars, not film characters to plug products. And certainly not a nasty villain for

The Britannia commercial: 'Kids couldn't get enough of Gabbar or Glucose.'

children's biscuits. J. B. Singh, the marketing director of Britannia, was one of the skeptics. But Britannia research showed that there were no negatives associated with Gabbar, and Alagh finally converted Singh by taking him to a nearby theater. Gabbar's allure was too powerful to

175

resist.

Javed Akhtar suggested using Gabbar's introduction scene for the advertisement. The script was done by a team from Lintas advertising agency, and the commercial

was shot by ad director Kailash Surendrenath. Amjad, Macmohan and Viju Khote were assembled at a quarry on the road to the Mumbai airport, and the Sippys loaned out the costumes and guns. Kailash knocked off the commercial in two hours.

'The Britannia commercial parodies Gabbar's "Kitney aadmi the?" introduction

The commercial, which parodies Gabbar's 'Kitne aadmi the?' introduction scene, was a sensation. Instead of running out for refreshments, people actually walked into theatres to see it. Even the usher at Minerva stopped his work to see the commercial each time it was screened. The biscuits were advertised as 'Gabbar ki asli pasand.' Kids couldn't get enough of Gabbar or Glucose. Sales doubled. And the pundits and critics were proved wrong again, as they usually are. The 'chooha' was outshining all the 'maharathis'. What many had dismissed as the film's weakest spot had become its hottest selling property. Amjad was overwhelmed by the response. This was beyond anything he had imagined. With every passing day his stardom grew.

The newly crowned number one villain bumped into Danny at a busy intersection in Juhu. Danny was going in the opposite direction when he saw Amjad drive by in his Ambassador. Danny waved him down. Danny had never met him before but he hopped into Amjad's car and congratulated him on a job well done. A crowd quickly gathered. Before driving off, Amjad thanked Danny for giving up *Sholay*. 'Otherwise,' he said, 'I would have remained an assistant.' And Danny in turn thanked Amjad. Post, *Sholay*, Amjad was quoting the unheard of price of eleven lakh rupees. Taking a cue, Danny, who till now was getting approximately six lakh rupees, hiked his price to ten lakhs. Even though he hadn't work in it, *Sholay* had benefited Danny too!

Several months later, Asrani ran into Amjad. Both had been invited to inaugurate a studio in Gujarat. On the flight, Asrani laughed: '*Haan ji,* did you miss the bus?' Amjad broke into a broad grin. The studio was about forty kilometres away from the airport. While driving there, Amjad's son felt thirsty, and they stopped at a small roadside stall. It was a ramshackle place selling cold drinks, biscuits and cigarettes. There was no other building or even a hut to be seen for miles. As they entered the shop, a voice crackled on a rickety gramophone: '*Kitne aadmi the?*' Gabbar Singh's dialogue boomed through the shop. The stall owner served the group their drinks but did not recognize the star. For a minute, Amjad stood absolutely still. His eyes squinted in recognition of his own voice. Then, listening to his voice playing in a shanty on a dusty, deserted road in the middle of nowhere, Amjad Khan sat down and cried.

YAAD RAKKHUNGA, TUJHE YAAD RAKKHUNGA

Sholay ran for more than five years. At Minerva, it played in regular shows for three years and then in the matinee for two years. Even in its 240th week, it was houseful. The Sippy's discontinued it only because Ramesh's next film, *Shaan*, was ready for release. Folklore has it that black marketeers at Minerva bought apartments and put taxis on the roads with their earnings. Dharmendra often told this joke: 'An NRI returned to India after several years. He asked a friend what had happened while he was gone. "Nothing, yaar," the friend replied, "*Sholay* is still running in the theatres and *Razia Sultan* is still being made in the studios."'

Sholay had captured the imagination of the entire country, but, ironically, at the *Filmfare* awards for 1975, Hindi cinema's biggest hit was deemed worthy of only one award. *Deewar* swept the awards that year.

Salim-Javed won the Best Story, Best Screenplay and Best Dialogue awards for *Deewar*, but nothing for Sholay. Javed still jokes that writers must never do too much good work in one year. Yash Chopra won the Best Director award for *Deewar*, and Shashi Kapoor was the Best Supporting Actor. From the *Sholay* team, only Shinde went home with a statue, for Best Editing.

But *Sholay* had no rivals at the box office. It stayed in the race long after the others had packed it in. It grossed approximately thirty-five crores of rupees in its first run; *Jai Santoshi Ma*, the other box office smash in 1975, grossed approximately six crores. One hundred and ninety prints of *Sholay* were made in the first year. Polydor sold over 500,000 records and cassettes, jacking up the ten-crore-rupee music market by fifty per cent on the dialogue sales alone. *Sholay*'s box office record remained untouched for nineteen years, till *Hum Aapke Hain Kaun* was released in 1994. Assessments of the size of *Sholay*'s audience are difficult, but G. P. Sippy believes that the film's total global audience till date equals the population of India.

Unlike other blockbusters, the film refused to fade away. *Sholay* became Bollywood's most successful re-run product. It has been released in Minerva more than five times since 1980, and each time the hall was packed. In fact, the last run was originally planned as a two-week stop-gap arrangement between releases, but it stretched into a six-week run in matinee on public demand. The

industry used to joke that whenever the Sippy coffers
started to dip, they would run *Sholay* at the nearest
theatre, rake in the money and start another film.

In 1982, when *Sholay*'s re-issue rights came up for
sale, they were picked up for an unprecedented fifty lakh
rupees. And the successive years did not dim its allure. In
1987, distributors shelled out the same price again for the

rights, and in 1992 it was sold at the film's original selling
price of Rs 22.5 lakh. Over 900 prints of the film were
eventually made, and even today approximately sixty are
in circulation. The Rajshris, who still hold rights for
several territories, estimate that *Sholay* has quietly
completed repeated golden jubilees.

On 26 January 1996, the film was telecast on Doordar-
shan and watched by large audiences. It is a guaranteed
viewer-magnet for the cable television operators, who

have re-run it innumerable times. Distributor Suresh
Malhotra likens it to the Taj Mahal: 'Every few years
there is a new generation who come to see it.' Distributor
Shyam Shroff agrees. 'As they used to say about the
British Empire,' he observes, 'the sun never sets on
Sholay.'

But works of art that acquire iconic status cast long
shadows. With time, *Sholay* grew larger than the people
who created it. As Orson Welles couldn't escape the
classic *Citizen Kane*, Ramesh Sippy couldn't escape
Sholay. But Ramesh never capitulated to *Sholay*'s
success. He defied audience expectations, and instead of
rehashing the *Sholay* formula, chose to always
experiment. The team followed Sholay with *Shaan*, an
urban James Bond-style caper about two petty thieves.
Shaan was a technically polished product, which
recovered its money but fell short of expectations.
Ramesh's next film, *Shakti*, an intimate portrait of a
tragic father-son relationship, was praised for its craft
and award-winning performances. As was the next
venture, *Saagar*, a lyrically shot romance. Ramesh then
moved his sights to television and created the small screen
classic *Buniyaad*. A partition soap opera, *Buniyaad* was
so popular that streets from Lahore to Mumbai emptied
out when the show was aired.

Salim-Javed split. Through the seventies and early
eighties, they fashioned the trends in Hindi cinema,
churning out hit after hit: *Chacha Bhatija, Don, Trishul,*

Dostana. Though none of their later works could recreate the magic of their early films like *Zanjeer, Deewar* and *Sholay,* they had already made the Hindi movie writer one of the central figures in the movie-making business. Their names were prominently displayed on hoardings, and their payment ultimately reached an unheard-of sum of Rs 21 lakh per film. In some projects, Salim-Javed shared up to twenty-five per cent of the profit. No other writer in the business has ever matched their success.

But eventually the egos grew too big for the hyphen. In 1981, they parted ways and pursued individual careers as writers. Javed's creativity found expression in songs. His name can still be seen on hoardings, only now it's as an award-winning lyricist. Salim eventually married Helen and retired. His three sons, actors Salman and Arbaaz and director Sohail, carry forward the torch.

Amitabh Bachchan held on to superstar status for two decades. The uncharismatic underdog who couldn't get a film left his rivals eating dust. Nobody else even came close. He was ranked number one to ten. Amitabh survived a near-fatal accident on the sets of Manmohan Desai's *Coolie,* the debilitating disease myasthenia gravis, and a scandal-ridden plunge into politics. By the late 80s and early 90s, Bachchan's films were propelled purely by his star appeal. In 1992, the 'one-man industry' took a long holiday from films and returned three years later.

The lady of the lamps was among Jaya's last roles.

Engrossed in her children and marriage, she abandoned her career soon after *Sholay*. She returned in 1981 in Yash Chopra's *Silsila* and has since done the occasional challenging role.

Dharmendra and Hema Malini married in 1980. Amma's strict admonitions were no match for Paaji's charm. But Hema's image as a dignified dream girl was so strong that even though she became Dharmendra's second wife, she escaped vilification from both the press and public. The couple have two daughters.

Hari bhai died in 1985. He was only forty-seven, but a lifetime of unhealthy eating and drinking habits had caught up with him. Sanjeev Kumar never achieved the status of 'phenomenon' as Rajesh Khanna or Amitabh Bachchan did. In fact, toward the end, he had become increasingly careless about his looks. But his name was a standard for good acting. And unlike other stars, he wasn't bound by commercial considerations. He enthusiastically donned a gray wig to play the Thakur. For Sanjeev, always, the role was the prize.

His close friend Amjad died on 27 July 1992 at the age of forty-eight. Amjad was candid enough to acknowledge that a role like Gabbar happens only once in a career. 'From here,' he often said, 'the only place I can go is down. This cannot be repeated.' But Amjad became a leading villain and character artiste, playing parallel roles in hits such as *Muqaddar ka Sikander, Suhaag, Lawaris* and *Mr Natwarlal*. He also turned in a critically acclaimed performance in Satyajit Ray's *Shatranj ke Khiladi.*

On 15 October 1976, Amjad met with a near-fatal accident on the Mumbai-Goa road. Swerving to avoid hitting a boulder, he drove the car into a tree. The steering wheel went into his chest. He recovered from the serious injuries, but the drugs administered to him caused a serious weight problem. He ballooned dramatically, and soon the roles coming to him were comedies. But Amjad rarely complained. 'I've come with nothing and whatever I've made in this life is profit,' was his philosophy till his untimely death.

Even *Sholay*'s peripheral characters lived in the film's shadow. A few years after the release, an angry stranger accosted Jagdeep in a studio. Film-maker Shakti Samanta had been attacked recently, and Jagdeep was afraid that he was going to be the second victim. He started walking away hurriedly, when the man called out to him: *'To miyan kahan ja rahe ho? Mera role ada kiya aur mere ko hi nahin pehchaan rahe ho!* (And where are you going off to, sir? You played me on screen and now you won't recognize me!)' It was then that Jagdeep realized he was being stalked by the actual Soorma Bhopali. The man standing before him was the real-life forest officer who had inspired the character. Bhopali threatened to sue because the writers had reduced him to a mere wood trader. *'Poora Bhopal mere peechhe pad gaya hai ki tu lakdi ka dalaal hai.* (All of Bhopal accuses me of being a timber thief.)' Jagdeep got away from the man but not from the character. In 1988, he made a film called *Soorma Bhopali*, in which the cantankerous lakdiwalla falls in love with a dancer and follows her to Mumbai.

The '*Angrezon ke zamane ke jailer*' line became Asrani's trademark. In over a thousand stage shows, from New York to Ludhiana, he repeated his Hitler parody. The jailer was so much in demand that Asrani had a costume made and kept it ever-ready with a wig. Some filmmakers tried to recapture the magic: in Mehul Kumar's *Love Marriage* and T.L.V Prasad's *Chandaal*, the jailer made a comeback, but the films were too feeble to work. 'Even if you wake me up at two in the morning from a deep sleep,' says Asrani, 'I can say the jailer's lines.'

Viju Khote became Kaalia for life. Viju's son was only three when the film was released, and sometimes when people on the road recognized Viju and shouted, 'Hey, Kaalia,' the little boy would get angry. Viju would ask the boy to ignore it and the boy would protest, 'But Papa they are calling you Kaalia.' And Viju would patiently explain: 'It's okay, beta, we are eating our bread and butter because of that.'

As for Sambha, to this day Macmohan laments, 'I have lost my identity.' Even now people approach him for an autograph and look bewildered when he signs his name as Macmohan. They think his name is Sambha.

Dwarka Divecha died on 5 January 1978. He had been

drinking all night, and in the morning his wife found him dead. He was sixty. At an age when most men transit into comfortable retirement, Divecha found himself in the middle of a scandalous love affair with a woman young enough to be his granddaughter. *Sholay* had enhanced Divecha's professional reputation and ruined his personal life. While shooting *Shaan* at Rajkamal Studios, Divecha bumped into Kamlakar Rao, who had done second unit camerawork for *Sholay*. 'Have you heard anything about my personal life?' Divecha asked Rao. Out of sheer respect, Rao said, 'No.' Then, seeing through Rao's politeness, Divecha added, with an air of defeat, 'I only wanted a child.'

Sachin became a director himself. *Sholay* stayed with him, literally. When he refused payment for his work, Ramesh gifted him an air-conditioner, the first one Sachin had ever owned. *'Jab AC ki thandi thandi hawa aati hai,'* he says, *'mujhe* Sholay *ki yaad aati hai.* (When I feel the cool air from the AC, I'm reminded of *Sholay*.)' Two decades later, he paid tribute to his early mentor by making a parody of *Sholay* for a television programme.

Sachin wasn't the only one who took home a *Sholay* memento. On the film's diamond jubilee, the Sippys gifted a Fiat car to Dwarka Divecha. The main cast received gold bracelets crowned with a diamond stud. It was a fitting gift. Like the stone, *Sholay* is forever.

ACKNOWLEDGEMENTS

I would like to thank the entire cast and crew of *Sholay* for taking the time out to participate in this project. Also, Vikram Chandra for being the first reader; Samar Khan for helping to get out-of-station vignettes; Kevin Rego for facilitating interviews in London; Dinesh Raheja and Jitendra Kothari for support and criticism; Hussain Zaidi for helping me look for black marketeers; and Suketu Mehta for always assuring me that his writing process was more torturous than mine.

INDEX

A

Agha, Jalal 135
Akhtar, Javed 15-8, 22-9, 31,
    33-8, 47-8, 50, 55-6, 65, 68,
    71-2, 87-8, 93, 108-9, 114,
    138-9, 141, 147, 153,
    156-7, 163-4, 167-9, 176,
    180, 182-3
Alankar 76
Allen, Jim 122-6, 128-9, 133,
    139-41, 146
Andaaz 10, 12, 14, 18, 21, 30,
    67, 69
Anwar 68, 71, 73, 75, 131,
    134, 154, 165
Asrani 36-37, 93, 167, 177,
    186
Azeem bhai 115, 118-21, 123-4
Aziz bhai 46, 73, 125-6, 131,
    134

B

Bachchan, Amitabh 9-11, 19,
    29, 31, 33, 35, 39, 53, 58-9,
    63-5, 67-8, 70, 80-1, 85, 87,
    94, 97, 111, 129, 157,
    163-4, 166, 168, 183-4 (*see
    also* Jai)
Bakshi, Anand 29, 49, 51
Basanti 3, 5, 30, 65, 93, 97,
    100-3, 108, 128, 144-5,
    160, 174 (*see also* Malini,
    Hema)
Bhaduri, Jaya 19, 29, 32-3,
    39, 53, 55, 58-60, 64-5, 67,
    78, 89, 112, 139, 157, 163,
    166, 168, 183 (*see also*
    Radha)
Bhikoo 115
Bhopali, Soorma 3, 26, 28,
    37, 50, 71-3, 141, 174,

185-6 (*see also* Jagdeep)
Buniyaad 182
Burman, R.D. (Pancham) 29,
    47-50, 92, 143-5, 159

C
Chopra, Prem 54
Chopra, Yash 166, 180, 184
Chaurasia, Hariprasad 50
Commoro, Romo 122
Crampton, Gerry 122-3, 126,
    129-30

D
Dengzongpa, Danny 29, 33,
    35, 39, 52-5, 61, 177
Deewar 164, 171, 179-80,
    183
Desai, Manmohan 22, 110,
    183
Dhanno 3, 5
Dharmendra (Paaji) 11,
    29-31, 35-6, 39, 64, 67, 70,
    93-4, 99, 102-8, 111, 117,
    123, 129-30, 157, 179, 184
    (*see also* Veeru)
Divecha, Dwarka 42-5, 57-8,
    63-4, 66, 69-75, 77, 86, 95,
    102-3, 108, 126, 186-7

G
Ganga Jamuna 34, 38, 115

Grant, John 30, 122

H
Hangal, A.K. 32, 80-83
Helen 93, 135-6, 183
Hussain, Mohammad 115,
    120-1

J
Jagdeep 37-8, 71-2, 185 (*see
    also* Bhopali, Soorma)
Jai 3-5, 26, 28, 31, 39, 64, 73,
    77, 79-80, 95-6, 106, 112,
    118, 127-8, 137, 141-2,
    144, 160, 164, 174, 180
    (*see also* Bachchan,
    Amitabh)
Jeetendra 92, 104

K
Kaalia 3, 117-8, 120, 186 (*see
    also* Khote, Viju)
Kapoor, Shashi 13, 166, 180
Kappu, Satyen 56, 64, 116
    (*see also* Ramlal)
Khalish 33, 100, 107
Khan, Amjad 2, 54-6, 60, 61,
    64, 68, 85-8, 104, 109, 117,
    124-6, 138-9, 145, 153,
    157, 160-61, 167, 176-8,
    184-5 (*see also* Singh,
    Gabbar)

Khan, Salim 15-8, 22-9, 31,
  35-6, 38, 47, 55-6, 87-8,
  92-3, 108, 114, 136, 138-9,
  141, 147, 153, 156-7, 160,
  163-4, 167-9, 180, 182-3
Khanna, Rajesh 18, 184
Khanna, Vinod 38, 71
Khote, Viju 28, 117-20, 140,
  176, 186 (see also Kaalia)
Khote Sikkey 28
Kumar, Dilip 10, 18, 38, 160
Kumar, Rajendra 18, 160
Kumar, Sanjeev (Hari bhai)
  29-30, 32, 35-6, 39, 53,
  63-4, 67, 70, 104, 113, 149,
  151, 157, 163, 184 (see also
  Thakur)

M

Macmohan 4, 34, 64, 89, 154,
  172-3, 176, 186 (see also
  Sambha)
Malhotra, Suresh 67, 154,
  166, 182
Malini, Hema 10-11, 14,
  29-31, 33, 36, 39, 44, 53,
  65-6, 68, 93, 99-102, 104-6,
  110, 120, 128, 157, 168,
  184 (see also Basanti)
Maruti 141-2
Mehra, Prakash 22, 31, 58,
  159

Mera Gaon Mera Desh 38,
  41, 163
Mohan, C. 153

N
Nafrati 117-20

P
Panvel 130-31
Pereira, Dolores 1-3
Polydor 51-2, 150-1, 169-70,
  174, 180
Pran 31, 107, 163
Prasad, Pt. Shamta 144
Premnath 54

R
Radha 3, 64-5, 77, 112-3,
  143, 174 (see also Bhaduri,
  Jaya
Rajshris 58, 173-4, 181
Ramanagaram 42, 45-6, 63,
  65, 73, 95, 112, 123, 151
Ramlal 56, 115, 147, 151 (see
  also Kappu, Satyen)
Rao, Kamlakar 57, 187

S
Sachin 68, 79-81, 109, 142,
  187
Sambha 3-5, 34-5, 60, 89,

100, 102, 145, 154-5, 172-3, 186 (see also Macmohan)
Seeta aur Geeta 10-2, 18, 21, 27, 29-30, 32, 49, 104
Seven Samurai 7, 25
Shaan 179, 182, 187
Singh, Gabbar 2-5, 26, 30, 34-5, 38-9, 46, 53-5, 57, 59-61, 73-4, 76, 79, 85-8, 92-3, 100, 103-4, 117, 120, 138-9, 142-4, 147-9, 151, 170, 174-7, 184 (see also Khan, Amjad)
Sinha, Shatrughan 11, 31
Sippy, G. P. 8-10, 14, 17, 21-4, 29, 38, 47, 73, 89, 93, 100, 150, 154, 158, 163, 165, 180
Sippy, Ramesh 8, 10, 13-5, 22-3, 24, 30, 31, 32, 33, 36, 39, 40, 41, 42, 45, 47, 48, 52, 53, 54, 58, 59, 62-6, 68-9, 72, 73-8, 80, 82, 83-5, 86, 89, 90, 92, 94, 97, 100, 101-3, 105, 109, 110, 113, 115, 121, 122, 134, 135, 138-40, 142-3, 145-6, 147, 148-51, 153, 154, 156, 158, 163, 165, 169, 172, 174, 182, 187

T
Thakkar, D.K. 122-3
Thakur 3, 5, 25-6, 31, 35, 41-2, 46, 56, 62, 65, 73-4, 76, 112, 115, 117, 127, 130, 136, 142, 147-9, 151, 153, 174, 184 (see also Kumar, Sanjeev)

V
Veeru 3-5, 26-7, 30, 36, 39, 73, 79-80, 93, 95-7, 100, 108, 127-8, 136, 141-2, 145, 160, 169, 174 (see also Dharmendra)
Verma, Badri Prasad 115

Y
Yedekar, Ram 40-2, 130

Z
Zanjeer 11, 19, 22, 31, 33, 58-9, 164, 183